The Savvy Cat's Guide

To Old Fashioned Money Sense
& New Fangled Cyber-savings

I0487710

By Dr. Oliver Candelario Carmalita Catman, M.E.C.A.T.

Translated by Kelly Dittmar

BEATNIK CAT PUBLICATIONS 2009
www.thesavvycat.com

Please Note:

The information and advice contained herein comes from twenty plus years experience, as a wife and mother, looking for ways to reduce expenses, save money and live better for less. I do not purport to be a financial planner or tax advisor. I approach these topics as a lay person and strive to present accurate information. Any statements regarding taxes, benefits or insurance should be verified with the appropriate expert. The inclusion of particular stores or internet sites does not imply my endorsement of them, or their endorsement of this book. Retailers and promotional programs may vary where you live.

Kelly Dittmar

THE SAVVY CAT MOTTO

Cheat me once?

Shame on me;

Cheat me twice?

I'll scratch your eyes out.

WHO IS THE SAVVY CAT?

Everybody and his dog write books about managing money, so I certainly think it's time to hear from a cat. I started life out on the wrong side of the tracks, so to speak, and now I live in the lap of luxury. It is the classic rags to riches sort of tale, but I learned a lot about money along the way; what it means when you have it, and what happens when you don't.

I am a feline author and self-styled pecuniary advisor. Translated into less than plain English that means I aspire to further the financial edification of those mired in the misery of monetary distress. My first book: *POINTY SIDE OUT: How to Claw Your Way to the Top* (2004) established my reputation as a feline self-help guru. Given that lofty status I feel a need to impart my own furry brand of wisdom to a wider audience on other important subjects as well.

Today, the topic of money is hotter than hot, so it seems a logical focus for my latest work. My closest friends and family members refer to me as Dr. C., or Dr. Catman. After this book hits the streets I suspect that moniker will be revised to Dr. Cashman a.k.a. THE SAVVY CAT. Check out my website www.thesavvycat.com to keep up with my latest tips and news.

Despite my currently comfortable situation, I still count my tins of tuna daily, just like Scrooge counted his coins I suppose. I know what it's like to be hungry and need to feel secure about my next meal even now. Those stacks of cans filled with fishy goodness, packed in oil or spring water, make me feel wealthy indeed – add a 25 lb. bag of kibble and some pricey bottled water and I sleep like a kitten.

My drastic change of circumstance taught me a valuable lesson. By chance I stumbled upon an important truth – money cannot buy happiness, but not having to worry about money is priceless. Of course I may have heard that on a television commercial or something, but I digress.

I extend my sincerest thanks to my purrsonal translator, a.k.a. Kelly, for helping me with this project. She's spent 20+ years digging for deals; she reads, listens, and looks for goodies 24-7, and racked up thousands of dollars in savings. As a news and trivia hound; she loves being in the know and loves to research info on the net. I dare say I want her on my team if esoteric info is the topic. Family and friends call her first if they need to find cheap deals or anything else online. I also want to thank all the people who read drafts and offered valuable suggestions, especially SAVVY Dad, Debbie Bozanich, the Toys, the Linds, Sandi Hull, & Tina Nakayama.

I would like to thank my cross-species bro, G.W., for timely assistance and design software consultations and help. I luv ya man. You're one rockin' computer savvy dude.

Once again, I must dedicate this financial tome to myself, simply because I am the most amazing, tuxedo-clad puss that probably every lived - in my humble opinion.

Dr. Oliver Candelario Carmalita Catman, M.E.C.A.T.
THE SAVVY CAT

TABLE OF CONTENTS

THE SAVVY CAT MOTTO 3

WHO IS THE SAVVY CAT? 4

OF TUNA, 'NIP & HAIRBALL REMEDIES 10

THE POWER OF COMMON CENTS 11

WHY LISTEN TO ME? 14

THE BEGINNING 15

SAVVY CAT LIFE RULE 16

REPLACE WORRY TIME WITH PLANNING TIME 17

TAXED TO DEATH? 18

NO TIME TO BE A SAVVY CAT? 20

THE SAVVY CAT PLEDGE 23

BASIC SAVVY CAT TOOLS 24

ORGANIZE THE IMPORTANT STUFF 24

KEEP HOLD OF RECORDS THAT MAY HAUNT YOU 28

GO WITH THE FLOW 29

CREATE A FAMILY SPENDING PLAN 30

THE SAVVY FAMILY SPENDING PLAN 31

FSP WORKSHEET 32

NO LINE ITEM FOR SAVINGS? 33

I'D RATHER LAUGH THAN CRY 35

WHAT COMES NEXT? 36

WHAT IF YOU DON'T HAVE ENOUGH? 37

WHAT DO YOU NEED? 38

GET THE FAMILY ON BOARD 40

TRACK YOUR PROGRESS 41

GET HELP BEFORE THE BANK TURNS ON YOU 42

GOOD CREDIT MAKES LIFE EASIER & CHEAPER TOO! 44

GET A FREE ANNUAL CREDIT REPORT 45

DEBIT CARD DANGERS...46

ADD 'EM UP...48

FREEZE THE CREDIT..49

COOL OFF EVEN IN THE WINTER...50

CAN'T DO IT ON YOUR OWN?..51

LATE, PAST DUE, FINAL NOTICE..52

TEACH YOUR KIDS TO MANAGE THEIR MONEY..............................54

LOWER MY BILLS...PLEASE!!!!!!!!!!!!..56

PERIODIC REVIEW...57

ANNUAL BILL REVIEW/ AUDIT...58

LOOK FOR BANKING DEALS..58

DEALING WITH INSURANCE..60

CASH RULES – NEGOTIATE THE SAVVY WAY..................................62

CUT PRESCRIPTION COSTS...62

HEALTH CARE FOR THE FURRY SET...64

DON'T GET SHOCKED BY ELECTRIC BILLS, DROWNED BY WATER CHARGES, OR, BURNED BY HEATING YOUR HOME...65

ENERGY STAR SAVINGS...67

KEEP WARRANTIES HANDY...67

BUNDLE UP..69

HOT SOLUTIONS FOR TROUBLESOME CONTRACTS.........................71

CUT YOUR GROCERY BILLS...72

EAT THE SPECIALS..74

SAMPLE SHOPPING LIST..75

DISCOUNT MEAT, PRODUCE, OR BREAD DEALS..............................76

BE PREPARED...77

PANTRY INVENTORY & MINI-SHOP WEEK.....................................78

BROWN BAGGING IS CHIC..78

MAXIMIZE SAVINGS WITH COUPONS & SALES...............................79

TAKE ADVANTAGE OF STORE REWARD PROGRAMS...82

LOOK LOCALLY FOR SAVINGS 84

CHEAP FUN ABOUT TOWN..85

CUT COSTS ONLINE..85

FREE EMAIL ACCOUNTS..86

SOME SITES THE SAVVY CAT SURFS..87

MISERY LOVES COMPANY JOIN A GROUP 88

HOW TO FIND A CYBER COUPON OR CODE 89

HOW TO ADD A PROMO CODE TO AN ONLINE ORDER 90

CHEAP FILLERS FOR FREE SHIPPING & SAVINGS..91

REBATE YOUR WAY TO FREE PRODUCTS 92

SPEND MONEY MORE THAN ONCE 94

ONLINE REWARD PROGRAMS 94

YOU PROMISE WHAT? FREE MONEY FOR EDUCATION?.......................................96

PLAY THE SAVINGS BALLGAME 98

HOW MUCH CAN SAVVY CATS REALLY SAVE?...99

TREAT YOURSELF OCCASSIONALLY 100

FIND THE LOWEST PRICE FOR GAS IN YOUR TOWN...102

OFFICE AND SCHOOL SUPPLY DEALS 102

SAMPLE YOUR WAY THROUGH TSA 104

SAVING TO HELP OTHERS...104

CRAIGSLIST, 2 GOOD 2 TOSS, &FREECYLCE 105

CLOTHING DEALS..107

USPS SNAIL MAIL SECRETS 108

MOVING?...110

HOW TO GET THE LOWEST PRICE ON A CAR...112

FIND THE CHEAPEST CAR TO INSURE...114

BARGAIN WAREHOUSE FEVER...115

TRAVEL DEALS 116

GIFT GIVING AND REGIFTING THE SAVVY WAY 117

THE SAVVY CAT'S FINAL ADVICE 117

ONLINE RESOURCES 119

NOTES: 123

ENDNOTES 124

OF TUNA, 'NIP & HAIRBALL REMEDIES

The economy dominates the daily news, the price of kitty essentials such as catnip, kibble, and, I dare say, tinned fish march steadily skyward. Our humans whine incessantly about rising gas prices, falling house values, and skyrocketing food expenses too. News reports show inflation rising faster than a helium balloon, businesses slashing jobs, and foreclosure and bankruptcy filings exploding. Yikes!

The good old U.S. of A. can barely print moola fast enough to keep up with the bailouts. Makes me wonder if Fort Knox really contains that much gold, or is the government dealing in theoretical cyber cash? Those unemployed conspiracy hounds certainly have plenty to ponder nowadays.

Most folks assume cats could care less about economic issues. Words such as aloof, distant, snooty, and snobbish immediately come to mind when people describe the average pussycat. These tags ring true in most circumstances.

When it comes to money, however, we plump furry creatures appreciate the value of a buck. The direct exponential relationship between the money our humans have to spend, and the value and quality of food, medical care and ergonomic feline playthings we get, is plain to even a hairless, incontinent, and blind geriatric puss on its last leg.

In many households feeding kitty or doggy involves a big bag of cheap kibble from the local supersize warehouse club, a dish or two, and some fresh water. In my salad days I was happy for whatever I could scrounge or catch. I was a lean, mean hunting machine. I even tried to eat one of the neighbors when he scared off my avian dinner guest one day. I found his ankle to be a bit too tough, though, even for me.

$$$$$
Parisian
French 'Nip
Vintage 1920

Free
Granny's
Backyard
Cat Weed

Shortly after the ankle-biting incident, I adopted a local family and my economic situation changed overnight. Suddenly, I dined on tinned fish, and got showered with expensive toys and squishy faux-leopard sleeping pods. Of course it took very little time for me to adapt to this new way of life.

How you may wonder do my attentive humans afford all these glorious culinary delights and material trinkets? Though not especially wealthy, they just work their money and max every penny to the nth degree. They doggedly search for the best they can get for the lowest price. These people seem happy doing it, even enjoying it.

Impressed by this frugal thrift I decided to keep one eye open at all times to discover the big secret.

THE POWER OF COMMON CENTS

After days with little sleep I conclude no covert doings here; just a common sense approach to money. I prefer not to brag, but my SAVVY Parents managed to pay off college loans, car loans, and the cozy family home months and, in the case of the house, years ahead of schedule. These prudent planners diverted cash into retirement, plus the cross-species brother's college fund, long before it even got to their wallet.

What makes these folks different? Some may assume they must follow the teachings of some televised financial guru. Not so, the thing that sets them apart from the pack is attitude. A savvy, smart spending and savings attitude with a capital "A"!

These people educate themselves about money. SAVVY Dad reads Money Magazine and other financial rags each month. SAVVY Mom gleans cost-cutting tips from frugal living publications and websites. Together they monitor the news of Wall Street, and catch the odd financial show on television. Retirement and college savings, prepaying loans, and building long-term wealth top family priorities.

Each quarter when their investment statements arrive in the mail they tally gains and, more frequently of late, losses. They've seen the ups and downs of bull and bear markets. Their first adult foray into investing was the Friday before *BLACK MONDAY* in 1987. That first lesson involved a 30% loss in 3 days. It took time to accept the unpredictable ebb and flow. Now if they lose some money one quarter, "Oh well, easy come easy go, at least we are buying new shares low," they say. If things go up, on the other hand, it seems to lead to behavior not suitable to mention in my G-rated book. Anyway…back to the topic at hand.

The SAVVY Family lives on take-home pay – the bi-weekly checks you get after all the standard and optional deductions are taken. SAVVY Dad takes advantage of automatic savings plans offered through his work and deducts money for retirement, college, and emergency savings first, before it ends up in his paycheck.

PAY ADVISEMENT	THE SAVVY CAT	
Gross Pay:	BIG BUCKS:	$$$$
Standard Deductions: Fed Income Tax, Medicare, SS, Pension, Insurance		($$$)
Optional Deductions: Union Dues, FSA Retirement, Insurance, Savings		($$$)
NET PAY:	45% LESS BUCKS:	$$$

The practice means long-term savings get paid first, and these parsimonious folks choose to live on less than they make. The amount left after these priority payments gets stretched to cover the family's monthly bills and living expenses. If there's a bit extra I help choose whether it goes to eating out, a movie, new cat toys or general unplanned fun.

Even during tough times when cash was tighter than skin on an apple, this crafty duo figured out how to make it to the next paycheck. It seemed really tough at the time, but fortunately grocery stores did not accept credit cards to pay for food, only checks or cash. Otherwise, even they might have fallen into the trap so many families do now when they use credit to pay for groceries when cash runs short.

Just once they tapped into their normally, off-limits stash to secure $4000 from an IRA for a down payment on the cozy family home: which incidentally they paid off early in just 19 years. In the long run the family learned to rely on each other to get through tough times. Plus they learned something important about themselves. They LOVE finding deals.

In fact, these crazy kids get inordinate pleasure from paying as little as possible for just about everything from soup to cars. Sales, coupons, discounts, rebates and freebies excite them. They stoop to pick up spare change from the street and deposit it in a conveniently located change jar in the kitchen. They store aluminum cans in the garage and when they get a big load SAVVY Dad goes to the recycler to get paid for them in cash; "spot cash," as dear old Gamma Gladys would say.

Initially SAVVY Mom used a spiral notebook to tally monthly and annual savings, but she eventually upgraded the list to a computer spreadsheet. Rifling through stacks of receipts they note coupons, rebates and freebies, then, add it all up.

The high-fiving, cheering, and chest thumping reminds me of drunken revelers at some he-man sports event. Yet, they cheer pennies, nickels, dimes, quarters, and dollars off the cost of everyday things such as bread, toilet paper, gas, long-distance fees, oil changes, and so on.

You can imagine the excitement the first time the tally totaled $1000 off expenses in a year. The other day SAVVY Mom met a store clerk who shaved $3000 off her own household's expenses last year. Those two thrifty gals ended up exchanging money-saving tips. I find this outrageous human exuberance baffling, but I certainly benefit from the game with cases of tuna purchased on sale at 2 tins for $1. I can't argue with that kind of fishy success. Combining research, price comparison, and the selective use of coupons, sales, rewards programs and rebates she proves it is possible to shave hundreds, even thousands, off the cost of everyday living.

SAVVY Mom ferrets out deals for insurance, internet, long distance phone plans and the like. She joined online rewards programs earning free cash for college plus numerous free gift cards ($5-$100) to places such as Red Lobster, Starbucks, Target, Shell, and Home Depot. In addition, the family gets free airline tickets, hotel rooms, and rental cars using points from their credit card and airline rewards programs. The size of savings varies with the amount of time involved, but even minimal efforts pay out when added up annually.

Perhaps equally important, I observed another fundamental long-time trait Savvy Mom and Dad rarely spend money without a plan. They budget and track where every penny goes. Every dollar counts and, they want more for less. Each year they review costs and expenses and use the information they gather to make informed decisions regarding expenditures for the coming year.

In our home not spending is fun; building wealth a reason for celebration. Living within one's means? What a concept! Today that seems impossible to many. Living below one's means, although common years ago, is now foreign to many adults and young folks weaned on a diet of easy credit, too much stuff, and instant gratification. Not so surprising lay-away plans made a big comeback this past holiday season as retailers offered cash-strapped consumers a way to purchase gifts without starting the New Year laden with high-interest credit card debt.

Clearly, we expect a lot of our dough. Talk, talk, talk and plan, plan, plan always comes before spend, spend, spend. Some people think SAVVY Family cares only about money, but happiness comes first. We view money as a means to an end, that is, a way to enable us to live life as we wish. Money means freedom; the freedom to do what we want, spend how we choose, and answer to no one. They are the captain of their own ship; I dare say. I love to be in charge, but as a cat I prefer not to be on a ship, bobbing in the swells. I am a land lubber, but I suppose saving money does not necessarily involve a lot of water, so I am sold on their careful ways.

I made a solemn vow to share this knowledge with the rest of the cats in the hood. For the first time I can give back to all the little people who struggled along with me eking out a paw to mouth living day to day. This one's for you, Frank.

WHY LISTEN TO ME?

Why not? Have those TV and government finance talking heads helped you? If you are drowning in debt or struggling to keep your head above water, I doubt their big money advice seems all that relevant to the average person. I don't suppose you run in to too many of those Wall Street honchos cashing their big bonus checks in the line at the bank in your hood either.

Surviving the month with bills paid, food on the table, and a little cash left over is the bottom line for many families. Everyone needs some basic financial savvy to survive in this crazy world. Young or old understanding money; how it works, how to get it and how to use it are basic lessons we all need to learn.

Old fashioned organization, curbing spending, and getting more for your money means even more today than ever. As you read I will also show you some new ways to use internet resources and cyber methods to save some of the green stuff, cash, money, coin, or whatever you call it, off the cost of just about everything from soup to nuts and electricity to gasoline.

I suppose some humans might find it intimidating to turn to a cat for advice, but humans in many cultures revere felines. I find the ancient Malaysian belief that cats ease the soul's journey from Hell to Paradise especially intriguing. Supposedly, Malay kitty killers were forced to carry and stack as many coconut trunks as the cat had hairs.[1] I suppose this is just a quaint local legend, but can you imagine how many coconut trees would fall to pay for the untimely death of just one unfortunate puss? Just my furry rump could wipe out several groves easily.

The moral of this story...turning to a cat for help, comfort and leadership in times of great human crisis, even times of economic calamity if you extend the analogy, seems sensible, even smart. Every financial guru has to start somewhere, so here I am. I will part the waters of monetary confusion and lead you from the Hell of financial disorder to the Paradise of fiscal organization and self-reliance.

Do I have your attention? I hate to resort to the claw. Of course, if you read my first book you already know I have no trouble slicing and dicing those who stand in my way, especially if a good deal is at stake.

THE BEGINNING

Necessity, the saying goes is the mother of invention. The same is true of our family's deal hunting ways. Trial and, sometimes error, can both be instructive in this regard.

SAVVY Mom originally started looking for ways to trim costs twenty-odd years ago. Faced with a new mortgage, young baby, car payments, and school loan repayments, money was tight. At the time, twenty dollars stretched into a week's worth of groceries through careful planning, coupons, and shopping the sales at multiple grocery stores.

The family used shampoo and other products free after rebates from Walgreens, Rite Aid and other stores. In those early years we ate whatever cereal that was less than $2 a box and planned menus using the advertised specials on sale at the local groceries. We nixed brand loyalty and tried whatever products cost the least. Rarely were we disappointed. Although, I must admit my delicate palate suffers with the tinny aftertaste of bargain-basement fish by-products, but without opposable thumbs I'm must rely on the staff to select and serve my meals.

Still we enjoy making a game out of cutting costs. If you can find pleasure in frugality it seems less like a sacrifice. In our home the cross-species bro believed Santa brought not only presents, but a fully decorated Christmas tree. The shock and thrill caused him to fall over the first year. No one bothered to mention that trees are free on lots late Christmas Eve so SAVVY Dad waited 'til dark, hopped into his economy pick-up and filched one. It seemed like magic to the boy, but saved us $20+ a year, and remains a treasured family memory.

When allergies nixed that sweet deal SAVVY Mom waited until New Year's and picked out an artificial tree on clearance at Target for $19.99. Hose the dust off that baby and you have instant tree ready to decorate come December. The per-annum cost of that reusable beauty drops yearly as a bonus. I dare say when the folks are in their dotage that little miracle tree will look just as good as the first Christmas it graced the living room.

Speaking of holidays, the stars and stripes go on sale after the 4ᵗʰ of July. Our red, white and blue display may have cost 90% less than one purchased the week before, but we are still 110% proud to fly that flag, topped with its glorious plastic, golden eagle finial, on every patriotic holiday. You can bet it did double duty this January when the Martin Luther King holiday preceded the historic inauguration of President Obama. God Bless America for producing a long-lasting synthetic fabric that is quick drying, resists fading and economical too!

As our income grew, deal hunting evolved from a necessity into a hobby, a money-making hobby I might add. Eventually SAVVY Mom learned how to search cyberspace for deals and found numerous ways to save online too.

You my dear reader, can benefit from the tips, techniques, and resources we utilize regularly. Your results may surprise you. You may even take up high-fiving, cheering, and chest thumping for especially good savings. I guarantee you will recoup the modest cost of this book with your new savvy ways. [Of course, that is simply just a rhetorical guarantee in case you are the litigious type.]

Everyone yaps about reducing their carbon footprint. I say forget those dirty toes, reduce your cash print instead. Why pay one penny more for food, services, and living expenses than you have to. Use these tips to reduce the cost of everyday living. This book is not about spending money; it is about living as well as you can within or, preferably, below your means. Of course if you can do it green too that's a bonus.

SAVVY CAT LIFE RULE

Before we get started let's get one thing straight. You alone are responsible for your lifestyle and living expenses. Whether you are male or female, a teen, a single parent, a married couple or an old geezer like me, the same principles apply.

If you spend more than you have or more than you earn, it will catch up. At some point the money runs out and you have unhappy creditors at your heels, whether it's your friend who lent you money for that new CD, your landlord, or your bank.

Do not expect others to bail you out. If you need a helping hand for a short time, food banks, social services, churches, your family or friends might be short-term emergency resources. Be wary, however, if that leg-up becomes a crutch and you become dependent on other people to support you.

That sounds harsh, but bridging the gap with money from family, friends, or other sources only prolongs the inevitable and generally ends up hurting those relationships. Plus, you will likely begin to believe the excuses, sob stories, and justifications you employ to convince others of your apparent victimization by forces beyond your control. Some day the help inevitably stops, and you are still on the same financial cliff one day, one week, or one month from disaster.

Also, when you accept cash handouts from any source, or accept loans you can never honestly repay, you lose your independence. If people provide you with money they pay for the right to tell you how to spend it. If you do not want to play by those rules, figure out how to take care of the problem yourself.

Your financial circumstances may not be entirely your fault you may have a run of bad luck, such as a divorce, medical expenses, job loss, etc. But for good or bad, each of us has to work with the hand we are dealt. It may not be fair, it definitely isn't fun, but the only solution is to address your situation, stop making excuses, and begin taking deliberate steps to educate yourself and improve your financial life.

REPLACE WORRY TIME WITH PLANNING TIME

Do you worry about money? I don't necessarily worry, but I certainly think about the cost of fresh and tinned fish. Six days a week my morning nap gets disturbed by the splat and banging noises that accompany the daily postal delivery.

I believe bills land on the floor with a louder thud than the rest of the snail mail. Some days it seems the kaboom sounds like bomb blasts. Those days I worry. I worry about rising kibble prices, and the cost of catnip, hairball remedies and veterinary care.

How much time do you spend worrying about bills, cash flow, or rising costs? I know I worry most in the still of the night when all but the nocturnal creatures such as cats snore loudly.

How much time do you spend actually doing something to change your situation? Probably about as much time as I spend cuddling with the beagle next door, zero, zilch, zip, nada, none, or never.

Instead of worry time spend some time each day working to understand your finances and gain control over your money. You may still wake up at night, but it will be more likely to swat your snoring bedmate rather than panic about bills, because you know you took charge, have a plan and are working to improve your financial life.

Some people find it useful to set a goal. You may want to put money into an emergency fund; save for a down payment on a home; set aside money for a car repair or insurance payment; attack a mountain of credit card debt; help kids headed to college; or you may just want to make it to the next paycheck without resorting to credit cards, payday loans or borrowing from relatives. Once you set the goal use the techniques in this book to help you achieve it.

Remember Great, Great Grandcat was right, a penny saved is a penny earned. It's also a penny you can use for something else. The small changes you make today will add up to big change by the end of the year. CHA-CHING!!! This is simple math, not rocket science.

I dare say, the rumble of more high-fiving families may fool those Richter scale techies into thinking the big one is about to hit. At the very least they'll wonder why people break into spontaneous smiles and glad-hand strangers more regularly in their neighborhood.

TAXED TO DEATH?

Three little words strike fear into the hearts of even the bravest among us. They are, IRS (Internal Revenue Service), taxes, and, purhaps the most heinous of all, audit.

SAVVY Cat feels no different. My poo is some of the most patriotic on the planet, but paying one cent more in taxes than necessary really twists my trousers the wrong way. Throughout the year I spend quite a bit of time in my purrsonal office reading tax code and looking for legal ways to keep my money in my pocket, and out of Uncle Sam's.

The inevitability of taxes rivals that of death. We rely on our city, county, state and federal governments for numerous necessities of life – postal service, roads, schools, police, electricity, etc. ad infinitum. (That's fancy talk for "loads of stuff" for those who failed Latin.) Income, property, use and sales taxes will

How much can you save?
Go to www.irs.gov *and check it out.*

never go away, but there is no shame in trying to mitigate the financial impact on you and yours.

Talk to your employer's benefits person for info on tax-advantaged flexible spending plans for medical and childcare expenses. See if they offer FSA (Flexible Spending Account), HSA (Healthcare Savings Account) or a child care savings accounts. Just be sure to plan the amount you commit to these types of accounts annually. Most plans only allow changes once a year during your employer's designated open enrollment period. At the end of the year any unspent money in FSA and/or child care accounts is not refunded to you. Rules for HSA accounts may vary depending on your circumstance. Verify rules and eligibility with the appropriate authority.[2]

Mind these cautions and these plans allow you to use pre-tax dollars to establish an account from which you are reimbursed for copayments, prescriptions, over-the-counter drugs and medical supplies, child care expenses and so on. That means you reduce your taxable income for tangible products and services you pay for already. This even includes commonly purchased items such as bandages and antibiotic ointment.

If you have a child in a licensed daycare, kids who need braces, you need glasses or dental work, or know you will have a one-time large planned medical expense talk to your HR representative and find out the details. These programs generally have pre-set annual limits and the amount you are eligible to contribute should be verified each year.

Depending on your tax bracket the savings might be several hundred dollars per $1000 diverted pretax. That adds up to free money if you think about it. If you don't take advantage of these programs already and you are eligible, you are throwing money away.

If you can contribute pre-tax dollars to a 401k retirement plan give until it hurts or you max out your allowable annual contribution. Keep track of work-related expenses throughout the year. Save receipts and find out if you may qualify to deduct unreimbursed expenses for mileage, travel, professional licenses, etc. If you are among the lucky few who still get occasional lump-sum bonuses, check if you will save on your tax bill if you defer that bonus to the following calendar year.

If you are retired keep track of medical expenses, save receipts, and try to group non-emergency procedures or health-related expenses to meet IRS thresholds for deductible expenses. One SAVVY Senior friend chose to postpone the purchase of a new hearing aid until 2009 because her projected medical expenses would qualify her for a bigger deduction than 2008.

For those of us saddled with rug rats, kids, or college students tax credits abound. If you do not understand what deductions your kids net, be sure to ask a professional. Again, keep track and save receipts. In some situations tuition and books can be deducted so don't miss out. Don't assume the standard deduction is the best. SAVVY Dad spent 6 hours checking out options on college expenses and netted a bigger refund by comparing various tuition expense deduction plans.

As far as sales taxes go, being savvy by comparing prices, using coupons, and buying items on sale or with a discount reduces what you pay. If you lower the price of a new appliance by 10% by waiting for a sale, you save dollars off the final sales tax, which gets calculated on the final sales price, not the price on the sticker. Just think a sale, a coupon, a rebate, rewards points and tax savings rolled into one.

SAVVY Mom just pulled this deal off when her dryer died. The dryer she selected went on sale for $567 which shaved 10% off the regular price plus $5 off sales tax. The cost of delivery, required parts and installation pushed the initial outlay up to $709. That total gets dropped by a $65 delivery charge rebate, and a $100 new credit card purchase rebate deal. Add a $17 cash back rebate because she made the purchase online by clicking the store link at one of her preferred shopping portals at www.fatwallet.com. So the net price plummeted to $527. I call that a Grand Slam in my ballpark!

That deal got me off track about taxes, but you get my point. Anyway, taking the time to figure out how to reduce the taxes you pay is not illegal, unpatriotic, or bad. It's smart.

NO TIME TO BE A SAVVY CAT?

I don't have time to find ways to trim costs or look for deals you say? To that I say, "There is no time like the present."

Do you pay a monthly fee for a checking account or an online bill paying service at your bank? If so, check out the free checking and bill pay deals that abound. Five dollars a month savings on banking services adds up to $60 by the end of the year. Online bill pay saves one postage stamp per bill, another $25 or so by the end of the year.

Is your cellular plan costing you an arm and a leg? Ten dollars a month savings on phone service adds up to $120 by the end of the year. Are you paying too much for long distance service? SAVVY Cat recently helped an elderly neighbor shave $8 a month off his long-distance bill, or $96 saved a year just by comparing plans offered by two different companies in our area.

Does your grocery bill resemble the national debt? Fifteen dollars a week savings on groceries adds up to a $780 savings by the end of the year. Purrhaps you need insurance, a new washer, an apartment, or want to learn how to save money on water and energy usage? Numerous web sites can help you compare products, services, and prices before you run around town. Take the time to check things out. You may just save big bucks.

What savings opportunities does your employer offer? Many companies serve up a cafeteria plan of benefits and that is not a lunchroom discount.

You may even work for a company that offers to match a portion of your contribution to a retirement plan. Although extremely rare today, if you have this benefit take full advantage of it. Free money rarely drops in your lap in this day and age, unless you hit the big one at the local casino's slots. Although money spent gambling disappears just as fast as paper flushed down the toilet, better to deposit the bits and pieces into savings and build a real nest egg.

Some employers will match your charitable donations dollar for dollar. You give $10 to your favorite no-kill animal shelter, fill out the appropriate company form, and your donation essentially doubles to $20. Some companies will do this for each and every donation you make to a legitimate non-profit organization up to certain limits.

Does your employer offer a discounted or free bus or train pass or offer parking discounts? SAVVY Dad, a county bureaucrat, drives his truck to the local Park & Ride and rides to work using his employer's free public transportation pass. That little benefit adds up to $8/day when he takes the train, $6/day for the bus. That amounts to as much as $40 every work week. Compare that to the cost of driving yourself and that little subsidy equals big, big money. Multiply the annual savings times the 21+ years he's slogged off in the dawn's early light and the sum boggles my mind.

As medical costs rise, employers find that healthy employees cost a lot less to insure. You might find your workplace offers reduced cost memberships to health clubs, free nutritional counseling, or other healthy living services. Who knew the employee handbook could be such a scintillating read?

Start paying attention to how, when and why you spend money. Are you a closet gossip monger who buys tabloids at the store checkout? Do you buy designer coffee or eat out frequently? Does stress at work or home send you running to the closest mall? Do you buy junk online just because you can't sleep?

"But I only buy things already on sale," you may protest. I say a sale is not savvy if it costs you more in the end. Paying with a credit card you do not pay off in full each month equals no deal. Worse yet, buying something on sale with money you need to pay your rent, electrical bill, car insurance or other essentials is just plain foolish.

Think about take-out, splurges or impulse buys. Estimate how much you spend weekly on stuff, multiply by 52 (the number of weeks in the year for you Mensa flunkies) and see what that spending costs over a year. Surprise, big bucks!!! Frittering away $6 a week on junk comes to over $300 a year.

Once the shock wears off you may realize you would rather cut back, or even eliminate some of those impulse purchases and use the money you reclaim to pay off a bill or reduce debt. SAVVY Cat likes a new catnip mouse once in a while, so even I recognize everyone needs a treat now and again.

Cutting back on some of those little bits a dollar here, twenty there when added together can be a substantial figure. That money may make the difference between staying debt free; may enable you to pay cash for an unexpected car repair, might allow you to purchase school supplies without using a credit card, might help pay down a car loan, your mortgage and so on. If you are lucky it might even mean a trip to Hawaii versus a trip to your backyard puddle pool.

No time to be a SAVVY Cat? I think not. SAVVY spending gives you power over money. Your money should work for you, not worry you. Take THE SAVVY CAT PLEDGE today! Even if your results are modest you will learn the thrill of taking charge of your money, and, ultimately your life.

THE SAVVY CAT PLEDGE

I solemnly swear to make my money work for me.

I pledge to organize my bills and financial records; eschew temptation (unless it's an enormously SAVVY deal I can pay in cash); to research prices; to plan ahead, and to make every cent count.

From this day forward I pledge to live within my means, to aspire to a sterling credit score, and to avoid the shame, embarrassment and outrageous cost of payday loans, bank overdrafts, and rent to own deals.

Henceforth, I shall be called a SAVVY CAT, and as such I vow to stop meowing about money and to take charge of my purrsonal financial future.

BASIC SAVVY CAT TOOLS

What do you need to be a SAVVY CAT? Regardless of your age you need the desire to educate yourself about money. You also need to commit some time to organizing your important financial records. In our abode, SAVVY Dad maintains a precise filing system that would likely rival that of the FBI, CIA, NSA or even the IRS. If you need to know our utility bill from June 1988 he can locate the original bill and check stub in seconds.

Assemble the following basic office supplies. I bet you will find most of the following items in your home. No need to spend a dime for anything fancy, just use what you have at hand. Remember every penny counts and you may as well start here.

Find a clear, secure spot to store your mail, sort it, and a quiet, orderly place to use for bill paying and other financial tasks. Even if you have to box things up to keep your important financial files separate from your general household stuff, do it. Just be consistent and, in time, it will become routine.

- ✓ Calculator.
- ✓ Calendar
- ✓ Folders or large envelopes
- ✓ Highlighter
- ✓ Notebook
- ✓ Red, blue and green colored pencils or pens
- ✓ Plastic Storage Container or File

You do not need a credit card (although it helps). You do not need to clip coupons (you can if you want). You can access the internet at the library and do research for free (just remember to log-off when you finish using a shared computer). You must make a modest investment of time to practice these strategies but the methods take less effort once you learn the ropes.

ORGANIZE THE IMPORTANT STUFF

Keeping track of your money, how you spend it and where it goes requires some simple organization. In general, orderly people know how much money they have, where their records are filed, and what upcoming bills need to be paid and when. If chaos, confusion, and clutter describe your household this may be a part of your financial problem as well.

What do you do with store, ATM, or debit card receipts? Do you toss 'em? Do you stuff them in a drawer only to unearth them to try to match them to purchases listed on your monthly bank statement?

Do you record checks and other payments in your check register and place the receipts or paid statements in an envelope or file until your bank statement arrives and you reconcile it? Or, do you ignore everything and resort to praying there will be enough money in your account to cover the checks you just wrote or the ATM withdrawal you just made?

You may think you have cash just because the ATM spat out $40 or your debit purchase got approved. But think about it, no financial institution can instantaneously update its records 24/7. It may take minutes, hours, or even a day or two for that transaction to post to your account. The second it hits your account the cash needs to be available or the toll in penalty fees may eat up your grocery money for the rest of the week. I view kibble and water as prison food, not cuisine.

Do you track your spending online? If so, do you check your transactions regularly and keep track of how much money you have in your account? If you use an ATM frequently, do you remember to subtract that amount from the total you have in the bank? Do you keep track of various ATM fees or banking charges you incur? Do you even know how much your bank charges for special services or fees? If not, find out pronto before you learn the hard way.

How often do you find yourself slammed with overdraft charges, bounced check penalties, or late fees? Overdraft rules vary by bank, but some charge upwards of $30 per occurrence and allow multiple overdrafts to stack up daily. The resulting mess costs you lots of cash. It also means future deposits get sucked up into the black hole of fees seconds after they touch your account, which compounds your headaches, not your interest.

Many folks ignore the fact that writing bad checks is a crime. Banks rarely prosecute probably because they make so much money off these sorry customers. Some banks will forgive the fees if an otherwise good patron makes an honest, one-time mistake. I suppose that happens about as frequently as I get an iced tuna latte delivered to me by Starbucks, but I sent them my address just in case.

If you suffer from chronic overdraftitis, planning, organization and money management must be addressed pronto or sooner. Handing money to the bank for avoidable fees is about as smart as burning money on the front lawn. Although I know some folks keep shoveling good money after bad simply because they refuse to acknowledge the problem is theirs to fix.

SAVVY Grandparents shared some of their purrsonal time-tested organizational tips. It pays to listen to these old cats once in a while. Here is what they advise:

1. Sort your mail daily and separate the bills.
2. Open each statement the day you receive it and, circle or highlight the due date in red.
3. Check the specific charges and fees on each bill. Confirm the charges are accurate. This is especially important with credit card statements. If something looks unusual check it out.
4. Place the statements in a folder or envelope labeled **UNPAID BILLS** in big bold red letters.
5. Log the payment due dates on your calendar in red. This may also help identify the most logical payment schedule because you can see where the bill falls in relation to your pay periods or the dates you receive regular income. You may want to color code pay dates in green ink. If you do this consistently you will find you can see ahead of time when and where your cash needs to go. Use this information to allocate money for food, incidentals, etc.
6. Mail payments seven to ten business days prior to due dates to avoid late payment fees or penalties.
7. Place paid bills in a folder or envelope labeled **PAID BILLS** in bold black letters.
8. Record payments in your check register by hand or on the computer. Again debits (money going out can be red) and credits (money coming in) can be green.
9. Every month or so sort the paid bills and file them by category and year to help keep track of spending and potential tax-deductible items.
10. Once a month check your bank statements against your own register to confirm all payments and fees are accurately recorded.

Use these same methods to track how you spend your cash or record debit purchases. THE MOST IMPORTANT THING TO REMEMBER IS TO RECORD EVERY WITHDRAWAL OR PAYMENT IN YOUR CHECK REGISTER, OR KEEP TRACK OF THEM AT YOUR ONLINE BANK SITE. SAVVY Nana emphasized this advice when she reviewed my book. Of course I listened since that seventy-something chick suffered just once from the shame of a bank overdraft. The sting of that mistake still felt some fifty years hence.

You should know exactly how much money you have available in the bank at any one time. If you do not know that information and can't figure out how to find it, ask for help and learn how to do it.

SAVVY Cat also recommends you keep a separate tally of late fees, overdraft charges, etc. At the end of each month look at that total, if it is more than zero you need to review how, when and why you incurred those charges. At the end of the year calculate the total amount wasted on unnecessary bank fees.

What happened? Did you lose track of the amount of money in your bank account? Did you mail a bill payment too close to the due date for it to arrive on time? Did you neglect to pay the minimum due or skipped a payment altogether? Find out where you went wrong and learn from that mistake.

If you find you are repeating the same mistakes time and again, you need to stop and examine why. It is your life and your responsibility. You need to face the facts: late payments and overdrafts are your fault, not the fault of the mailman, the bank, or anyone else.

If you continue to deny there is a problem, despite the evidence before you, or if you make excuses for repeated late payments or overdrafts, you may need to ask someone to monitor your bill payment and spending. I know that sounds like loads of fun, but forget your pride and embarrassment and get help today. Stop flushing money down the toilet. Remember this is money you need for anything from groceries or medicine to retirement. Planning to drop dead on the job won't get you off the hook, I might add.

Organizing your finances eases the burden of managing your money. Put your receipts in one place and sort them into files monthly. While you are at it, make extra folders for your pay stubs and tax forms. Get in the habit of following the same payment and recording routines time after time, and you will slash wasted money on late fees, overdraft penalties and charges. You will know how much money you have, where you spent it and can produce receipts or proof if necessary. It also simplifies finding records for taxes. You may even find some extra tax deductible expenses as a bonus.

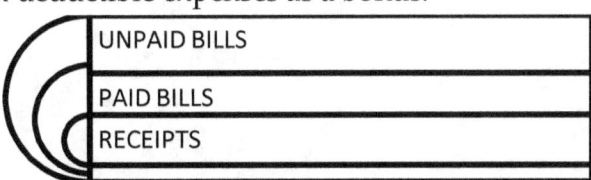

KEEP HOLD OF RECORDS THAT MAY HAUNT YOU

How long should SAVVY CATS keep those pesky files? Each person knows their own comfort level for keeping personal records. SAVVY Dad, for example, keeps most everything financial permanently including paystubs, bills, bank statements, checks, etc. That is fine with me so long as I am not expected to file this stuff each month. If you hang on to the files long enough you won't have to deal with them at all, it will be your heir's problem. Depending on how much you love said progeny you might view this as payback for all the trouble they caused while you were alive.

I decided to check out the legalities of how long one should keep old financial records. Here's what I found at www.bankrate.com.

TAXES - 7 years. (Returns, Cancelled Checks & Receipts documenting deductions)
IRA CONTRIBUTIONS– Forever
RETIREMENT ACCOUNTS – Annual Summaries Forever, Quarterly 1 Year
STOCK/BOND PURCHASES – From purchase to sale, plus 7 years for tax documentation.
CHECKS – Keep records related to mortgage, major purchases, investments, retirement & taxes at least 7 years to permanently. Shred non-essentials after 1 year.
BILLS– 1 Year in general, 7 years or permanently for taxable items, investments, mortgages, etc.
PAY STUBS – 1 year
W-2 FORMS – 7 years or longer.
MORTGAGE RECORDS – Permanently.[3]

When the time comes to dispose of purrsonal records and information, a sturdy crosscut shredder works better than my claws. If shredding becomes a chore see if your bank sponsors a regular monster shred day. My SAVVY Credit Union holds a member event every quarter or so. They hire a big industrial strength semi-trailer shredding system. You get to watch as your purrsonal records get dumped into the jaws of cross-cut paper slicing death. A free, cheap thrill for the family, just make sure the kiddies stand clear and keep their paws in their pockets.

GO WITH THE FLOW

Do you get surprised and anxious about annual, semi-annual or quarterly payments for insurance, taxes, or other large bills or expenses? Those bills used to spin my blood pressure to the moon when they arrived in my post box.

Being the SAVVY Cat that I am, I looked for a cheap solution to this stressful problem. For some strange reason I thought of SAVVY Dad, the sewer engineer, and his immortal words of wisdom, "Go with the flow." Of course, he was referring to the use of gravity to move wastewater through pipes to treatment plants, but in that split second I could see that sewage and cash actually have a lot in common.

Following your cash flow can ease the pain of paying big nasty bills. If you know when the big bills arrive, and match those bills to the flow of your money, you can plan ahead for the odd times you know cash will be extra tight. Whether you get paid weekly, bi-weekly or monthly, this system helps you see when your cash arrives and what you need to pay before your next paycheck.

Fortuitously, the same day I had this monetary epiphany I received a free Humane Society Cat Calendar in the mail. I used it to make a simple monthly cash flow and bill payment chart. The fact that it cost me nothing simply added to the brilliance of the idea.

You can pick up a free pen and calendar at a lot of businesses. When you are at the bank, pharmacy, or the local shops see if they have giveaway pens or calendars sitting out for the taking. SAVVY Dad has quite a collection of pens, pencils, key chains, and other advertising goodies he's accumulated while out doing his business.

Use your free calendar to mark down when your monthly bills come due. Add your paydays, and the odd times big bills, such as property taxes or insurance premiums, are due throughout the year.

Give yourself an advance reminder note to plan for any monster bill's arrival. Try giving yourself 6 to 8 weeks advance notice. If that's not enough time to save up for the bill you might want to start earlier and set aside a smaller amount every payday. Store your calendar in the bill drawer and update it once in a while.

At the end of the year you'll have a record of your basic monthly cash flow. You may still find those big bills onerous, but at least their arrival won't be a foul surprise.

CREATE A FAMILY SPENDING PLAN

Getting through the month with food and cash left challenges many families. As costs rise, even small changes can mean the difference between surviving tough economic times relatively unscathed, or digging yourself deeper into debt by depleting meager savings or using credit unwisely to maintain a standard of living you think you deserve, or more likely, grew accustomed to living.

For many people, the word *budget* conjures up many nasty feelings including limitations, restrictions, and denial. It's time to rethink that negative connotation. Replace the B-word with a **F**amily **S**pending **P**lan (**FSP** if you like the moniker) and you gain **F**reedom from worry, **S**elf-reliance as an individual or family, and **P**ower over your money.

If you know how much money you make, plus the cost of your basic living expenses, you have the ability to make informed decisions. You will know exactly how much money you can spend on groceries weekly. You will know if you need to cut back, and by how much. You will know if things are so dire drastic measures are the only solution.

Everybody has a formula for creating a FSP. The SAVVY Cat is no exception. The plan gives you the cold, hard facts. The actual figures you need to know and understand in order to make positive steps toward financial solvency.

If you feel overwhelmed, ask for help learning to handle your finances. Your bank, library, church, human resources department at work, or local social service agencies are good places to start. In my town dialing 211 connects you with the United Way of Pierce County, Washington and their free resource and referral services. The front of the phone book usually lists available community services too. You may even have a friend, family member or neighbor who would be willing to help you as well. SAVVY Cat likes some of the following online sites too: www.aetv.com/bigspender; www.betterbudgeting.com; www.clarkhoward.com; www.financialplan.about.com; and www.wesabe.com.

A FSP may not be pretty. This isn't the time to play ostrich and stick your head in the sand. Include all regular income or payments you receive. Likewise, be honest about debts and obligations. Many of us underestimate how much we truly owe in non-

THE SAVVY CAT'S GUIDE

mortgage debt. Get those figures in black and white, add them up, open your eyes, and take charge.

The FSP is a planning tool. Do your best to calculate accurate figures. You can find the information from bills, your bank statement, money order receipts, or drugstore and grocery slips. If you can't find this information go to your bank and ask for an account printout. Many banks will help you sort out your checking account if that means you stay current and avoid fees.

The numbers may scare you, but you are not alone. I dare say most people will find loads of room for improvement. Knowing the enemy (your actual cost of living) gives you power – the power of conscious choice. It doesn't beat the power of the claw, but for humans, it's a start.

THE SAVVY FAMILY SPENDING PLAN

The following breakdown reviews income and outgo. This plan focuses on take-home pay or net income. That is the figure you get to spend after taxes, Social Security, and other deductions.

It should include any monthly income you routinely receive regardless of whether it is taxed or not, that may include child support, rental income, disability payments, etc. You need to create as accurate a financial picture as possible.

This process will also help you determine if you make enough money, or if you need to earn additional income to bridge the gap either short-term or permanently. You may have to move to slash housing costs, use public transportation instead of a car, sell personal items, or consider other severe cuts. Do not include emergency support from any source in your plan. The whole point of the FSP is self-sufficiency.

The worksheet is based on one month out of twelve. You may wish to break your plan down further to match bi-weekly or weekly paydays if that makes it easier for you to manage your money.

Freedom Self-sufficiency Power

FSP WORKSHEET

Income:	
Take home Wages or Salary	
Child Support	
Social Security	
Pension	
Interest Income	
Rental Income	
Insurance Income	
Disability Payments	
TOTAL	
Priority Expenses:	
Housing (Mortgage or Rent)	
Food	
Water/Sewer/Garbage	
Heating	
Electricity	
Child Care	
Prescriptions or Medical Deductibles	
Health Insurance	
Basic Phone Service	
Car Payment	
Car Insurance	
Vehicle Gas & Maintenance	
Rental/Homeowners Insurance	
Life or Disability Insurance	
Other Loan Payments	
Credit Card Payments	
TOTAL	

Other Expenses:	
Banking & ATM Fees	
Cellular Service	
TV Service	
Internet	
Dining Out, Take out, Lunch Out	
Entertainment	
Clothing	
Gifts	
Contributions	
Subscriptions/Club Dues	
Other Allocations (Emergency Savings, Repairs, Vacation, etc.)	
No Clue Where It Went*	
TOTAL	

*NO CLUE WHERE IT WENT?

SAVVY Cat advises carrying very little cash. When you purchase something use a check, a debit card, or a credit card (the latter only if you pay it in full each month). That way you will have a second record of what you spent, in the form of bank or credit card statements, in addition to your receipt. That's a savvy back-up plan to keep track of cash that may fall through the cracks if you misplace the receipts or forget to write withdrawals into your check register. Plus you can check statements anytime online and keep track of your cash and know how much you have at any given time.

NO LINE ITEM FOR SAVINGS?

You will notice that there is no category on the worksheet for savings. SAVVY CATS deduct cash automatically from every paycheck before it gets into their purrfectly manicured paws. Out of sight, not missed in the pocket I say. Aspire to set aside some money each month in addition to your automatic deductions. That paycheck money can be used to save up for an upcoming bill, gifts, or maybe even an inexpensive mini-vacation.

Even if you only withhold the minimum amount to qualify for automatic deposit, say $25 per pay period, by the end of the year that is $300 or $600 set aside with little or no pain, suffering, or deprivation depending on if you are paid once or twice a month. Add any pay raises or bonuses to your deductions, because if you are managing to get by on what you currently make you can bank the raise, and watch your money grow.

If your employer offers a tax-deferred retirement plan, sock as much as you can afford up to the maximum annual amount allowed. In 2009 the cap for Tax Deferred Retirement Savings (TSA) maxes out at $16,500.[4] After age 50, the feds allow you to put even more into those accounts. Talk to your Human Resources Department today. Reducing your income means reducing immediate taxes. Even if you can only do a small amount each pay period, that adds up to money saved in taxes on April 15. Of course you will eventually pay tax on the withdrawals in retirement.

The sooner you start saving the more money you will have to use in the end. Look for more information at www.irs.gov. SAVVY Bro started a Roth IRA at age 19 saving $100 a month. If you choose to make automatic debits from a checking or savings account, many companies will accepts payments as low as $25 a month. That's just a week of fast-food lunches or super mocha latte's if you think about it. Not such a painful sacrifice even for a young adult.

SAVVY Mom and Dad used this simple bit by bit strategy to make savings a priority even during times they struggled financially. This method represents a step toward learning to live on less than what you make. That is the key to building your nest egg, or in my case an emergency tinned fish fund. As a matter of fact, you probably won't really miss the money if the amount starts out small and gets deducted without thought each and every month.

This same process can be used to pay down loans or save for a big purchase. An extra $25 a month on the mortgage decreases the principal owed and shaves dollars off the interest you pay in the end. If you get a raise or some other windfall earmark a small amount to debt repayment or savings. At the end of one or two years or longer you will start to see the small change add up to big bucks.

Just remember to build a little fun into the mix. All work and no play can set the stage for impulsive, and potentially expensive, spending. SAVVY Dad always makes sure to earmark a small portion of any raise for a little unstructured fun. The SAVVY Cat plans on buying a new faux-leopard sleeper with my piece of the pie.

www.irs.gov

I'D RATHER LAUGH THAN CRY

Have some fun with this painful money stuff. Saunter up to your neighbor knowingly and say, "I have a FSP do you?" They may act puzzled, but they will likely assume you snagged one of the latest techie toys, and congratulate you. They may even feel a bit jealous because you obviously know something they don't.

Enjoy the moment- you've earned the license to feel self-righteous. If you like them enough you can share the secret of your newfound confidence, but it certainly isn't compulsory.

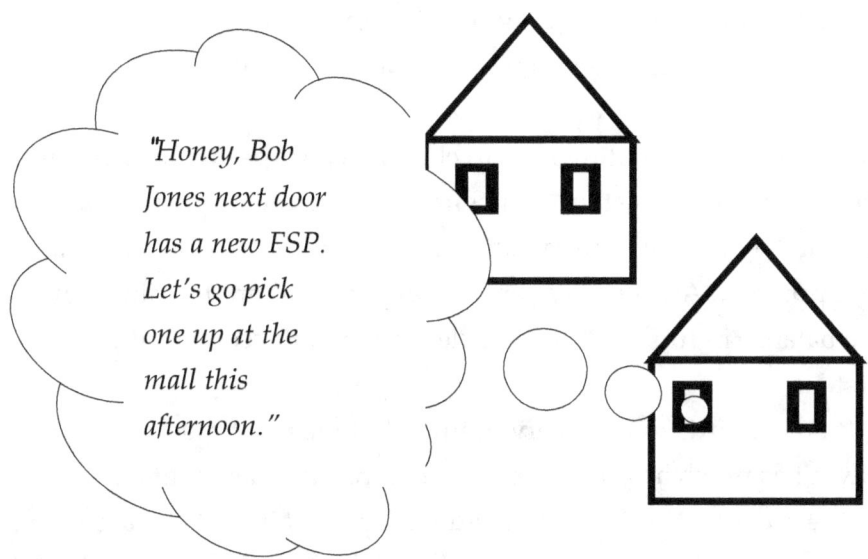

"Honey, Bob Jones next door has a new FSP. Let's go pick one up at the mall this afternoon."

WHAT COMES NEXT?

For me the next step would be a nap, but you will likely feel a great sense of accomplishment if you keep slogging along. The truth lies in the math. If the figure you get after subtracting expenses from income equals zero on up, ok. Now you can focus on improving your overall financial picture.

A negative figure signals hard choices ahead. Deficit spending, like good old Uncle Sam, spells disaster. Unlike Ol' Uncle Sam, remember you can end up in the slammer if you print up some cash. So unless you prefer three squares, a cot and roommates with names like Counterfeit Jake or Swindler Sam, figure out a legitimate way to make a living.

DO THE MATH:

INCOME MINUS TOTAL OUTGO EQUALS...

$49,750 - $48,650 = GOOD NEWS

$49,750 - $55,350 = BAD NEWS

Once you know what you spend versus what you make, use that information to devise a plan. Everyone can benefit from a monetary audit, reducing unnecessary spending, paying down debt, and ramping up savings. Getting the most out of your money means more than ever given the uncertain times. Now is the time for talk, talk, and more talk.

Sound strategies abound for deciding how to chip away at specific bills or build savings. Choose a method that works best for you. Some folks advocate paying off the smallest bill first so you can feel like you are making progress. SAVVY Mom and Dad take a slightly different approach. Always pay substantially more than the minimum due if you can't pay the balance in full, and then tackle the loan or account with the highest interest rate first.

Aspire to pay off credit cards in full every month. At times that may be not possible so focus on paying as much as possible over the minimum payment due and stop adding charges to the account. SAVVY Mom and Dad pay 'til it hurts by accessing their accounts online and transferring cash from their bi-weekly paychecks until the debt or loan is zero. They used that same strategy to pay off auto loans and our little brick abode.

Even if you can only afford an extra $5 or $10 that extra reduces the time you carry the debt and ultimately cuts the amount of interest you pay in the end. Once the debt is paid you can use a similar strategy to build up savings for upcoming bills, long-term needs such as retirement, or to build a stash for the inevitable emergencies.

Those less vigilant financially are charged for it. Avoid outrageous fees for overdrafts, steer clear of payday loans, and pay your bills on time. If you know you are going to have trouble paying a bill, the sooner you contact your creditor the better. Above all, honor your obligations. If you commit to paying $25 per month for a debt, do it without fail. If you find you are paying bills late, overdrawing your checking account, and begging relatives for money, you need a serious wake-up call.

WHAT IF YOU DON'T HAVE ENOUGH?

If your cash flowed out before the month did, your first task is to prioritize your immediate needs. Get a pen and paper then make a list. The most important expenditures, safe shelter, medicine, basic food, utilities, and child care, might top the "Pay First" column. Once you've covered those costs, itemize remaining obligations such as insurance, loans, etc.

The first step is to acknowledge your debt and address whether it is from poor spending habits, a job loss, a medical emergency, etc. Huge credit card debts, multiple car loans, a mortgage you can barely pay, signal attempting to live a caviar life on a tuna budget. In that case a lifestyle overhaul is in order. A lay-off or some other emergency event may be more temporary in nature and require a different approach to slashing non-essential expenses for a limited

PAYDAY LOAN DANGERS

Those tempting Payday loan businesses in your neighborhood and online lie in wait for the desperate. These legal loan sharks on TV look innocent enough, but beware. The difference between payday lenders and the guy you meet in the back alley is that those payday folks won't beat you with a baseball bat when you can't repay your loan. Their plan is even more insidious; if you can't pay their short-term loan they just charge more fees and roll your debt over into a new loan time and again.

These lenders must disclose your interest rate and fees up front, but interest rates charged may add up to 400% or more plus service charges. You need an industrial-strength magnifier to read the contract terms. Learn more about this nightmare and what you can do to avoid it at: www.ftc.gov and search for Payday Loans.

time.

Second, if you know you do not have enough money to cover specific bills in full, phone your creditors immediately. Ask to arrange alternate payment without delay. Make the first move. Do not ignore bills or avoid opening them, collectors are much less likely to work with you if you wait for them to track you down.

Many folks would rather get something toward what you owe than nothing at all. The same goes for purrsonal loans from friends or family. Creditors might be willing to let you skip one payment, they might reduce or defer interest or late fees, or they might be willing to take reduced payments for a short period of time. Just be sure to follow-thru with whatever agreement you make.

If you do not send negotiated payments as agreed, you will likely be asked to pay the account immediately, and in full. Do everything in your power to follow-thru; if you act like a deadbeat you will be treated as such.

Finally, use the cold hard facts you unearthed from your FSP to decide if you have no other choice but make long-term changes. If your problems are truly temporary, for example you have an unexpected medical bill or car repair, you may be able to cut back on some non-essential expenses, sell some personal items, or pick up some extra hours at work. Brainstorm ideas and keep up the talk, talk, talking.

WHAT DO YOU NEED?

Everybody talks about basic needs. What are they? The definition of basic needs depends on whom you ask. SAVVY Cat's list includes: a cushy blanket; adequate food (including fish), access to medical care and a dog- and toddler-free home. Your list will be different, but safe housing, food, clothing, education, health care and basic transportation of some sort are important needs for everyone in general.

Take time to educate yourself and your children about the importance of living within your means, the cost of your life, and the difference between necessities and desires. Although this sounds trite, knowledge truly is power.

Today, we've expanded our view of basic needs to include cell phones, cable or satellite television, computers, internet access, etc. Whether that is good or bad depends entirely on your economic situation. If the cost of the extras of modern life prevent you from making ends meet, time to re-evaluate what you consider to be basic needs.

See if you can identify some quick ways to slash expenses. Take the monthly totals for some of your discretionary categories such as dining out, entertainment, subscriptions, and the miscellaneous category of unknown spending, multiply each figure by 12 (the months in a year) and see what that tells you. Sometimes the amount spent in these areas seems small until you add up a year's worth of mindless spending.

What items can you live without for a short time? I could sacrifice buying a fresh catnip mouse for a few weeks in a life or death situation. Are there things you really could do without for a longer time or give up altogether? Can you do without season tickets to the ballpark? How about borrowing books, movies, or music from the library rather than renting or buying the stuff. Try giving gifts of your time or services rather than spending money on junk no one really needs. Use the cash you do not spend, even if it is only $5 a week to pay down debt, start a savings account, or set aside money for an upcoming bill.

One SAVVY Friend cut down on take-out. Her family typically ordered pizza on Friday night. They still had pizza, but cooked frozen pies for less than half the cost of delivered pizza. SAVVY Dad brown bags lunch four days a week. SAVVY Cousin unplugs appliances when not in use, grows his own veggies, and reuses bath water to flush the toilet. SAVVY Mom learned how to sell items on eBay and Amazon.com to make some extra dosh (that's Brit-speak for money for those who don't watch Bargain Hunt on BBC America). SAVVY Bro goes to the local name-brand beauty school to get a haircut with high-end salon style on the cheap. SAVVY BFF gave a friend 85 minutes of vacuuming for her 85th birthday.

Communication at home remains the key. Talk to your family, make this a team effort. You will succeed if you all work together toward a common goal. The bottom line is self-sufficiency. If you can pay your own way you can do what you want. If you can't meet your bills you either have to earn more money or cut your expenses.

Finally, use your FSP as an ongoing planning guide. Review it occasionally and update it as needed. As you pay off debts revisit your goals and decide where the "new" money goes. Be sure to plan a fun reward to mark each milestone. High-fives all around!!

GET THE FAMILY ON BOARD

Involve the whole family in these financial lessons. In our family the annual budget negotiations start in late December. The howling, crying, and hair pulling going on in our house over the holidays has very little to do with grooming me, and everything to do with negotiating line items in the annual family budget.

A financial planner once told SAVVY Dad to loosen up and take a modest vacation. That sage advice quite possibly saved a marriage and prevented a fight over kitty in divorce court. It also taught us a valuable lesson about working toward common goals. Taking the advice to heart SAVVY Dad booked a modest family get-a-way to Disneyland. SAVVY Mom conceded on a retirement savings issue and we all enjoyed ourselves in Anaheim.

The moral of this story is that finances are a family issue. Everyone working together toward common goals strengthens your bonds. You give your children a tremendous lifelong gift when you show them how to make sound financial choices no matter how difficult they may be. Share the power of self-reliance.

Children know if money is tight whether you tell them or not. They see you toss mail in a pile and never open it. They hear the conversations you have on the phone with creditors demanding payment. They hear you ask family or friends for "loans". They hear the city worker at the door asking for immediate payment or your water or electricity will be shut off. They see your frustration when the bank teller or ATM declines your request for cash. They may even offer you the money in their piggybank hoping it will help.

If you include your children in your financial life they will learn that everything we do has an associated price. It may help them avoid mistakes you made with money. Some think hiding this information keeps kids from worrying. It might, but in the long run not sharing real information about money, bills, banking, credit and the connection to how and the way we live, may hurt them for years.

Kids do not need to know how much you make, or the particulars of a troublesome bill, but they can understand that family money is limited; that the priority is to pay for shelter, food, and medical care. Also, they can accept that sometimes we have to say, "No" to things we want or delay getting things we need because first we must save up the money.

Tell the kids not to worry, but you need their help to get things on track. Tell them you have a plan and you need to work together to make it happen. You can explain that all families have different amounts of money each month to pay for things they need and want. Simply say that right now we need to use our monthly money for some of the most important family needs and talk about what those things are.

You may be surprised how aware your children are of your financial situation. Give them some credit and acknowledge how they can help you address these problems. They may even have some good ideas about what they are willing to live without in order to help the family survive the immediate crisis and build a better future.

Once priority bills are paid, you can offer your children a say in how remaining funds may be allocated. Elementary school age children can accept that we can't do everything we want and we have to choose between doing this or that.

If you know you can afford $10 for a weekend treat, or a car trip to the beach, or an inexpensive meal out, let the kids help decide which it will be. They will likely whine a bit less because they got a say in what to do, and they might appreciate the treat a bit more knowing it resulted from everyone pitching in, working together, and being responsible as a family.

TRACK YOUR PROGRESS

Make a priority list of your financial goals for the week, month, and year. Whether you want to pay off a credit card, catch up with late bills, or ramp up retirement savings write those goals down. Post the list somewhere prominent. Keep track of your progress.

Our Goals January
1. ~~Pay off VISA $875.~~
2. Save for car insurance $200/mo.
3. Plan for 2009 unpaid furlough.
4. Save for emergencies $50/mo.

If you get frustrated or tempted to chuck it all and hit the mall, go to the list and remind yourself of the goals, and your progress toward them. I like to slash the total with a claw as I make headway on a particularly troublesome payment, but you can use a pencil or pen.

When you pay off a long-term debt, bury the documentation in a file and tuck it away. SAVVY Dad files bills, bank statements, paystubs, tax information, etc. It is important to keep a record of payments just in case you need proof at a later date. File your stuff monthly and put it in a secure place along with your other important financial documents.

People talk about burning their mortgage when they finally pay off their house. You could celebrate other milestones such as unloading the college grads, paying off credit cards, etc. Never actually burn the real documentation, but you may hold a ceremonial bill burning. Please take appropriate precautions the fire department frowns on playing with matches.

Of course, some cheering and high-fiving is an entirely appropriate celebratory activity and not currently regulated by the authorities so far as I am aware. You may annoy your neighbors with your exuberance, but invite them to join in the fun.

GET HELP BEFORE THE BANK TURNS ON YOU

For some folks, their banking habits cause serious financial woes. Many schools no longer teach basic financial life skills, or parents neglect to educate their children about checking accounts, deposits, withdrawals, etc. SAVVY Mom knew a person in college who took his monthly bank statement, looked at the balance the bank said his account contained, and then wrote that figure in his check register. Unfortunately for him the balance in the statement was larger than the amount in his account simply because he never wrote down the amounts of the checks he had written in the interim. The bank soon wiped out his balance with overdraft fees and closed the account leaving him high, dry, and bewildered.

If you need help to understand the ins and outs of banking go to your bank and talk with one of the managers. They can show you how to keep track of your account on paper or online. Whenever family finances were tight Mommy knew exactly how much money she had at any time; she knew the exact second Daddy's paycheck would be deposited; and she calculated to the dollar how much was available for groceries each week. The key to surviving a crisis is vigilance and thrift.

ChexSystems

It's not cereal.

The banks and creditors levy outrageous fees for overdrafts and late payments, but those fees are clearly stated in your account information. If you do not understand the penalties and fees associated with your accounts talk to your bank. This is something only you can do. Making the same mistakes month after month makes no sense.

Have you ever heard of ChexSystems, Inc.? Very few people outside the banking industry have a clue who or what that is until they are told they can't open an account because of it. ChexSystems, Inc. is a consumer reporting and collection agency used by financial institutions. The banking industry subscribes to their service to avoid risky customers, those who repeatedly overdraw accounts, abuse debit or ATM withdrawals and/or owe fees or debts to banks, credit unions, etc.

Banks report poor risk customers to ChexSystems. They then use the same service to screen people who apply for new savings or checking accounts, loans, or credit. If you are listed, even by mistake, member institutions will not accept your application to open an account of any type. If a member institution refuses to open an account based on a ChexSystems report you can request a free copy of any report they may have. Any negative information can only be withdrawn by the reporting institution and can impact you for up to five years.[5]

Why do you think all those check cashing services thrive? If you find yourself regularly overdrawing your account resulting in heinous fees, provide false information regarding your income, or can't make good on the bank fees, you are playing with fire. People without checking accounts spend a lot of extra time and effort just to cash a paycheck or pay bills. The sad thing is that poor money management generally led them down that road in the first place.

SAVVY Mom once applied online for a Money Market savings account from a bank she used for her business checking and credit accounts. The application for the account was denied due to a supposed report on ChexSystems. SAVVY Mom nearly choked on her coffee and called her purrsonal banker at the local branch to find out what to do.

The bank manager looked things up and found nothing amiss. The branch opened the account and everything was fine. SAVVY Mom wrote for a report which confirmed all was well. Her problem was probably a typo on the online application form, but it certainly educated us about this little known entity lurking to make your banking life a living hell. When SAVVY Dad had a similar experience we knew exactly what to do; another typo, go figure.

www.ckfraud.org/chexsystems

GOOD CREDIT MAKES LIFE EASIER & CHEAPER TOO!

Credit impacts more than just your financial life. A good credit rating enables you to take full advantage of all the best deals whether they come in the form of lower rates for insurance, loans, credit cards or getting an apartment or cell phone. Arranging for bank overdraft protection, gas, water and electric service, hotels, car rentals, and airline tickets are all easier too.

It pays to understand credit. Three great websites to check out are www.myfico.com, www.bankrate.com and www.financial-education-icfe.org.

Good credit and low debt means I worry a lot less about my purrsonal medical expenses. I try to schedule any medical appointments with SAVVY Mom simply because I know her estimation of my monetary worth exceeds that of Dad. She also carries the most high limit plastic in her wallet, and would not hesitate to use those babies to pay for advanced life support services if necessary.

Did you know that people with good credit tend to be careful in other aspects of their lives as well? For good or bad employers, leasing agents, and insurers also use credit scores and/or FICO ratings, to assess whether folks will be good employees, tenants, and careful drivers. [For example, SAVVY Mom and Dad get a 10% reduction on their car insurance rates because GEICO charges less for consumers with excellent credit.]

If a credit bureau uses a category-based system your credit rating may sound like a cut of beef. The credit bureau, Experian, rates individuals with the categories of High Risk, Non-Prime, Prime, Prime Plus and Super Prime. Needless to say I am rated Super Prime ounce for ounce. Others may use your FICO score.

What's a FICO? At the most basic level, a FICO is the credit rating score assigned to individuals based on their bill payment and loan repayment history. Scores range from 300 (very bad) to 850 (almost too good to be true). They are used by lenders to calculate risk and have a direct connection to whether or not you will be offered credit and at what rate. The better your score, the easier it is to get credit and at the lowest interest rate currently available.

What does FICO stand for? SAVVY Cat investigated thinking it would be some important federal government office acronym name thingy. It's even more surprising than that. SAVVY Cat quizzed a Ph.D. in the family and found even highly educated humans have no clue about this. Those over 21 may use the following information judiciously to score free drinks at the bar on Friday nights.

FICO stands for Fair Isaac and Co. Who is that you ask? In the 1980's that company created the software used to calculate credit scores.[6] Who would have thought? I certainly didn't know that little factoid and I bet others have no clue too. Combine your free drink strategy with half-price appetizers at the local watering hole and you will have an entertaining and cheap night out. Just remember to designate a sober driver.

www.bankrate.com
www.financial-educationicfe.org
www.myfico.com

GET A FREE ANNUAL CREDIT REPORT

Once each year every citizen over 18 may view and print their credit reports free from each of the big three credit bureaus: Experian, Equifax Credit Information Services and Trans Union Corporation. There is no fee for the service at www.annualcreditreport.com. We do it around New Year's Eve. That helps us remember to take advantage of the service.

Unless you have an urgent concern about possible identify theft or plan to apply for a large loan don't pay for a credit report. Anytime someone denies you credit you have the right to contact the credit bureau in writing to get a free copy of your report detailing the specific reason you were declined.

Take the time to print and review your complete file free annually. If there are any discrepancies or there is incorrect information listed in your file you have the right to dispute or question the discrepancy in writing. Follow the individual credit bureau's instructions regarding disputes, and take time to confirm your report is updated to reflect the information you provide.

If you want you can pay a fee around $8 or so to get a copy of your FICO score. This report can be purchased from one or all of the three bureaus. SAVVY Cat orders one, reads what it says, and leaves it at that. The report you purchase will give you a number between 300 and 850 or a generic risk rating. The report also explains what factors impact your score- too much outstanding credit for your income, irregular payment history, and so on.

Before you sign up for one of those credit or identity protection services find out if you really need them. Some folks pay $10 a month or more for the so-called peace of mind. SAVVY Cat says monitor your own financial records, be smart about shredding documents you discard, make sure your mailbox is secure, and keep your money in your pocket.

If you plan to apply for a mortgage, buy a car, remodel a house or need educational loans check your credit report beforehand and take steps to raise your score. Credit ratings get assessed monthly. You can impact your score positively by addressing problems and paying bills on time. It may take months, a year, or longer, but the potential savings on interest can add up to hundreds or even thousands of dollars over the life a loan.

www.annualcreditreport.com

DEBIT CARD DANGERS

PIN – based debit cards offer the convenience of paying cash for purchases without having to write checks, use a credit card or carry cash. I purrsonally love them because they can be used in a variety of settings and you can use your bank statement to track spending without having to worry about missing receipts or go through stacks of paper to know exactly how much you paid for an item or service and where. When you enter your PIN number the amount is automatically authorized by your bank and deducted from your account, although this may not be instantaneous it is pretty darn quick.

Debit cards with the VISA or MASTERCARD logo can be used wherever these credit cards are accepted. You pay cash for your purchase, but don't use a PIN number, and you sign a slip of paper similar to a credit card transaction. Remember this is not a credit transaction it is an electronic cash transfer. You might find your bank blocks access to funds in your account in excess of the actual purchase made, to ensure you have the cash in your checking account when the debit posts, hours or perhaps days later. These holds may last for several business days or more depending on your financial institution's rules.

Be wary of using debit cards for gas, rental cars, hotel rooms, and other travel expenses. These transactions regularly result in funds being frozen. The amount blocked may vary, but in some cases the purchase price plus an additional $75 (gas) to $400 (hotel, rental car, etc.) might be unavailable to you until the transaction is verified days later. This protects the bank and the merchant, and guarantees you have funds available to pay for those services when they are due.

In the mean time you had better not spend that blocked money. If you do spend it, for example you write a check to pay your rent, and if you don't have extra money in your account to cover the hold plus the check you may end up overdrawn at the bank. OUCH!!!!

Rental car companies post signs at their counters which explain their policies for holding your cash hostage. Hotels will let you hold a room with a debit card, but ask that you use a credit card to pay when you check in, otherwise you will have a hold placed on your account for the projected cost of the number of nights you stay or a higher flat rate. Again, you might not have access to that money for days.

This could mean you don't get approval to pay for groceries, or you can't withdraw money from an ATM. Or, horrors, your checks turn into rubber balls bouncing down the street incurring late charges, and overdraft fees from hither to yon. That cheap weekend getaway may end up costing you more than a 5 star hotel in Paris, France.

Don't expect much sympathy from the bank. "But I swear I had more than enough money," you'll whine. You will insist you were never told about a hold and that your charges were much smaller than the amount blocked in your account. The dollar signs blinking in the Banker's eyes will tell you how much they care about your sorry predicament.

Avoid all of these horrors by asking lots of questions before you use your debit card. Ask your banker to explain their policies and the associated fees before your first purchase. When you travel and you have a credit card use that, but if you don't, you need to plan ahead to have excess cash available to cover holds that will inevitably be placed on your account.

Once again, communication is the key to avoiding this disaster. Be savvy and keep your money in your pocket. Plan ahead, pay attention and have a safe trip.

ADD 'EM UP

A friend I know has a saying, "If you can afford the monthly payment, you can afford the item." OK, but be sure to look at the big picture before you sign on the dotted line.

Why do you think so many stores and companies offer to break your payments into smaller monthly increments? The payments look innocent enough $25 here, $75 there and so on. Or they might offer to give you 10% off of your purchase if you open and use their store credit card. Car dealers are notorious for asking how big a payment you want on your car loan. How is it that they always manage to tailor the loan to make your payments equal the target amount?

Purrhaps they are nice? Maybe they hate to see people die of shock at the cash register when the total pops up? Possibly, they want to prevent a good customer from getting whacked by their spouse when they come home with the new super deluxe, bigger than it had to be computer, TV, car or the like? Perhaps they worry you will strain your eyes reading all that microscopic print detailing the terms, length and interest of your ~~loan~~ payment plan?

What these businesses want...what they really, really want...is to get you to agree to a deal that makes them loads of extra money. Once you add interest, monthly account service fees, etc. that big ticket item scores them loads more cash. If you use a bank credit card, or secure a loan to make your purchase, the bank gets the goodies because the retailer is paid up front.

If you plunk down cash I suppose the world might stop spinning. At the very least you will probably get to lug that super deluxe flat screen to your car by yourself. Ignore those murmurs of "Cheapskate" and remember to note the workout on your exercise log when you get home.

If you choose to go ahead with the monthly option, you may find that one month the extra payment is easy to make, but the next month you don't have enough cash to pay it, because you have a quarterly tax bill due. Just remember to add up all your small monthly payments along with all the other obligations you have. The FSP and the simple monthly cash flow calendar become mighty handy here.

Give the 90 days, 18 months, same as cash deals the same close scrutiny. If you are extremely disciplined it might work, but if you are late on one payment, or can't pay the item in full before the due date, all the accrued interest and fees will get tacked on because you didn't fulfill your end of the contract. Plus that bargain deal just got a lot more expensive.

Better to gamble on a savings account and pay cash later. Plus that gadget thingy will cost less because they need to make room for the next greatest model at the big fancy showroom. Watch out or you might get suckered into hauling that new monster TV home. Self-control is your word of the day.

FREEZE THE CREDIT

Credit cards muck up the lives of many folks. If those little consumer fulfillment aids, almost literally handed out like candy by stores, banks, gas stations and so on, fill your wallet take stock. Get out a pencil, paper, and your SAVVY Cat calculator and add up all you owe. Then write down the interest rates you are being charged on balances you carry month-to-month.

Many people take out cards with low teaser rates and then forget the interest shoots up to double digits after a few months. Or if you are late or miss a payment your interest is quickly reset to a higher level, plus you are charged another outrageous late fee too. Some card issuers do not credit payments immediately. So even though your payment arrived in their mailbox on the due date, the company may not post the payment to your account for another day or longer. I bet a case of tuna that they don't hesitate to assess a penalty too.

If the amount owed on any card is more than you can pay in full that month, put those tempting pretty plastic cards on ice and figure out your next move. Give yourself a time-limited breather, perhaps one week but no more than two. In the mean time, even if you pay only the minimum amount due on each of your cards, mail your payment 7 to 10 days before the due date. If you know your payment won't make it on time you can call and give the card issuer your bank information over the phone. You will likely be assessed a processing fee, but it is usually much smaller than a late penalty and won't result in your interest rate being reset.

If what you owe on credit cards resembles the national debt take immediate action. SAVVY Cat knows some folks advise that you pull out big shears and slice the plastic, but that tactic works best on TV. Cutting up the cards or closing the accounts may do more harm than good in the long run. You may end up doing that, but wait until you clearly understand the long-term financial implications.

So before you do anything rash, take your credit cards, place them in a plastic bag and seal it. Place the bag in a large container, fill the container with water, but remember to leave a little bit of room at the top for expansion before you seal the lid. On the outside of the sealed container tape another plastic bag with $5 cash and a piece of paper on which you have written the following instructions: "To be thawed in case of emergency, but only on a day which has no 'y' in its name, otherwise take the fiver, suck it up, and thank your lucky stars you have $5 to your name." Toss the lot into the freezer and walk away.

At the end of your self-imposed freeze-out be honest with yourself. If the cards are too tempting, close all but one major credit card (VISA, MasterCard, etc.) and keep it in the freezer or put it in a safe-deposit box for emergencies only. An emergency on the level of a major car repair, the death of the fridge or some other unexpected catastrophic occurrence may qualify, but the grand opening of the new 80 gazillion square foot shopping mall does not.

The whole point is to think before you spend, to plan before you buy, and to recognize the consequences of your actions. If you do choose the freezer method however, do not risk frostbite by thinking for long periods while holding the icy container.

COOL OFF EVEN IN THE WINTER

Wait before you make a big purchase. Give yourself a cooling off time to think about it. Take a few days, a week, a month, or longer to evaluate the expense. I personally like to nap on it for a few days.

Join your credit cards in the deep freeze, or at least gaze upon them for a bit. Ask yourself is this something I need? Is this something I can wait to own? Can I find it at a discount, on sale, or used? Can I pay for this purchase in cash? If I do not have the money now, how long will it take to save up?

Just this winter I followed these steps when trying to decide whether or not to purchase a new electric blanket. Of course the fact I am toasting my pink pads on setting #4 tells you the answer I reached.

Depending on what you decide you can move forward with the purchase or not, but pat yourself on the back because you took the time to think it through and evaluate the pros and cons of spending the money. Sometimes just planning how to pay for an item is enough to turn you off of it.

SAVVY Mom and Dad used this technique with the bro when he was young. If he wanted to buy the latest computer game or gadget they insisted he devise a plan and wait until he had the money. Several times, at the end of this self-imposed waiting period, he decided he no longer needed or wanted the previously shiny, new doohickey; his attention usually shifted to something else, but by then he generally had the cash to pay for it.

CAN'T DO IT ON YOUR OWN?

If you know there is no way to bridge the gap between what you make and the cost of how you live the jig is up. You may need to move in with relatives, you may need to change jobs or careers, take the bus instead of owning a car and so on.

Your friends or relatives may be willing to teach you the basics of money management, but if you know you will not be comfortable sharing your financial details, or able to listen to their advice, consumer credit and employment counseling can help. An outside perspective can often clarify these highly emotional issues. Your local United Way, church, Better Business Bureau or State Attorney General's office can help you find reputable resources.

Many so-called consumer credit counseling services are more interested in making money off you than helping you. Before making any decisions, or signing a contract, ask lots of questions.

The experts at www.myfico.com suggest consumers find answers to the following before choosing a financial counselor or agency.

- ✓ Call the State Attorney General's office to confirm the agency is a licensed, registered non-profit with an unpaid Board of Directors.
- ✓ Check if the group is affiliated with or accredited by any independent organizations such as the National Foundation for Credit Counseling or the Council on Accreditation. Anyone serving as an advisor or counselor should be a Certified Consumer Credit Counselor.
- ✓ Find out if they offer free classes on general budgeting or finance, or if they offer only debt management plans to consumers near bankruptcy and buried under high credit card debt.
- ✓ Determine if clients meet with an advisor in person, in a group setting, by phone, or online.
- ✓ Confirm the fees charged. Set-up fees of $50 or less and monthly fees around $25 are typical.
- ✓ Verify they work with all creditors, not just those who agree to pay them a fee.
- ✓ Ask if advisors receive compensation for writing up debt management plans, or if the agency keeps any portion of your first or later payments as a fee or, a so-called, donation. Also make sure any money you give the agency goes to debt payment and is protected from misuse or fraud.[7].

Whew! I need a nap just to recover from thinking about all that stuff.

LATE, PAST DUE, FINAL NOTICE

If you get contacted by a collection agency regarding a debt you may owe, arm yourself with information, make a plan, and know your rights. The government regulates the collection industry.

The Fair Debt Collection Practices Act provides consumers with protection from illegal, aggressive or intimidating collections practices.[8]

If someone calls and claims you owe them money, request they send you information in writing documenting the original debt, the amount owed, the relevant

Check out www.FTC.gov or call their consumer hotline toll-free, 1-877-FTC-HELP.

dates, etc. Be sure to get the address of the collection agency as well. Write this information down too and keep a record of the date and time of the call.

Do not be coerced into giving anyone your banking or credit card information over the phone. Even if you know you owe the debt, wait to get the written verification so you can double check it against your records. Remember, bill collectors may not use abusive language, call you at unreasonable times, or threaten you with arrest or other scary consequences. You can write the collection agency and request they no longer call your home with regard to the debt in dispute.

Although it seems unreasonable, collectors may even try to contact your relatives, neighbors, or employer and try to locate you. They may not tell anyone other than a spouse about the reason for the inquiry and they can't try to collect payment from the other folks. The unsettling tactic most likely results in your relatives or boss getting on your tail to get the bill collector off theirs. The impact on your job and relationships may linger longer than the debt.

Now it's time to do your homework. Here's where your bill payment/filing system pays for the time and effort it took to set up. Go find the supposedly errant bill and confirm the information the collector told you was true.

> ✓ Assemble the proof, receipts, check copies, etc.
> ✓ Check the dates. Is the bill current? If the debt is more than three years old check the statute of limitations in your state. Even if you acknowledge that it is your debt, you may not have to pay the debt if it is older than the set statute of limitations. I would hope you make good on all debts, but you make that call.
> ✓ If you find proof you paid the debt you have to take charge and write the collector and the original debt holder and send copies of your receipts, checks, etc. Be smart and send copies, **do not send the original documents**. Send the information certified mail with return receipt. That way you can prove the information was received, by whom, and when.

THE CHECK IS NOT IN THE MAIL

Stop with the lame excuses for being late or not having something to pay toward a past due bill, they've probably heard it all before. Just think, how many people claim Grammy just died, the car died, or the dog died.

Of course if you really want to throw those blood suckers off your tail tell them the cat just died. So few people think of cats as loyal cuddly creatures, they will likely laugh so hard that coffee will spray out of their nose, short out the phone and possibly electrocute the whole lot of bill collectors within their arm's reach.

If you do try this, remember it is just a temporary delay tactic. In this economy I suppose even bill collectors will have folks lined up to replace those hapless electrocuted skunks within hours, purrhaps.

✓ If you owe the debt, set up a payment plan and stick to it. Deadbeats deserve to suffer the consequences. No one gets a free ride in this world.
✓ Once you pay the debt, make sure you keep the receipts and payment details in your files. Don't get burned twice by being sloppy.[9]

www.ftc.gov

TEACH YOUR KIDS TO MANAGE THEIR MONEY

The lessons of money management should start early. If you receive cash or checks for your baby open a bank account and deposit the gifts. Do this at the same time you apply for your child's Social Security Number. Use those gifts to start a college savings account or to purchase a big ticket item like a car seat, stroller, crib, etc.

Toddlers can collect small change in a piggy bank. Teach those short sticky humans to scan for change while strolling, walking, or playing at the park. Their proximity to the ground and natural curiosity make them the ideal change hounds. Have them pick up any coins they spy and hand them to you.

When their piggy bank is full deposit it into their savings account at the bank. Many banks offer children's savings accounts. Frequently, they will offer a $25 bonus deposit to encourage kids to save. Our credit union even offers a club for kids and sponsors special kid friendly events at Halloween and other times throughout the year.

During the elementary years start teaching your children about how you make choices about how to spend money. Some parents give their children a weekly allowance. Others pay nickels, dimes, and quarters for specific jobs or chores. When it is your child's *payday* discuss what they will do with their money.

Some parents have their children divide the cash into four piles. SAVVY Mom's best friend taught her son place a portion (for example 25%) into a jar to give to their church or charity, another amount (about 50%) into long-term savings for college, and the rest could be saved or spent as he chooses. If your kids have trouble with the idea of divvying up the money, get four blocks. Help them divide their money into four equal piles one for each block and then make their allocations.

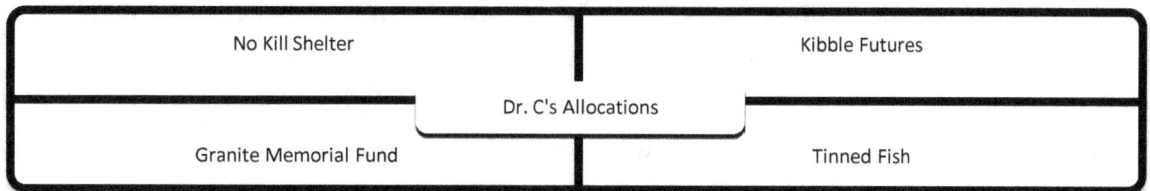

This is a great time to talk about how you divvy-up your paycheck. SAVVY Mom and Dad started talking to the cross-species bro when he was six or seven. They talked about where money goes after they got paid. They talked about paying the mortgage, food, utilities and other priorities. They talked about making choices about spending based on their current bills, what they needed for the family, and what things they might want to do or buy.

As children get older they can start setting aside money for larger purchases, a video game, clothes, or whatever. Middle school and high school age children can help save for college expenses, a car, or some other major outlay as part of their long term savings.

When teenagers get a part-time job talk with them about what they plan to do with their money. Share your successes and failures. No need to repeat financial mistakes from generation to generation. Also, take time to discuss how choosing a career or job involves many factors including your interests, education, monetary aspirations, and even the need for medical care, retirement or other fringe benefits.

Motivate your teens to save by offering to match a certain level of savings with an equal amount of money from you. When your child turns 18 go with them to the bank and help them open a free student checking account. SAVVY Bro got a checking account, checks, a debit card, and a low-value credit card with a $300 limit when he hit that milestone. He learned how to use the account, checks, and the debit and credit cards while he still lived at home.

The initial credit card limit was set after a discussion with the bank manager and a frank talk with the bro detailing a no bailout policy. At the time the $300 limit was an amount SAVVY Bro could easily pay in full each month using his savings from his part-time job. The bank raised his credit limit every six months as a reward for maintaining a responsible use and payment history.

When the bro started college he and the parents spelled out who paid for what and set a limit for how long they would offer support. SAVVY Bro opened a Roth IRA at age 19 using automatic withdrawals from his checking account to fund it monthly. SAVVY Dad offered to match whatever amount he saved dollar for dollar.

As the economy fluctuates so does his Roth IRA, once the shock of the ups and downs wears off he reconciles himself with the fact that investments must be looked at in terms of many years, not months. I suspect he will be happy he started saving at age 19 when those dollars grow exponentially over 40 year's time.

Taking the time to teach your child about savings, checking, credit, and other financial matters while they are still at home allows you to monitor their accounts, and gives them the opportunity to ask questions about bank statements, bills, credit, etc. What better way to prepare them for life's tough costs and ups and downs?

Those SAVVY CATS love to talk, talk, and talk some more. They also love to save, save, and save some more. Passing financial skills from generation to generation is a priceless gift that keeps on giving.

LOWER MY BILLS...PLEASE!!!!!!!!!!!

Although you may be living as carefully as you think you can, use the consumer resources available to check that your phone service, car insurance and other regular expenses cost you as little as possible. Savvy spending means doing some homework first.

I say research and plan before you spend unless you're richer than Bill Gates and can afford to throw money out the window. Although I believe he is a pretty savvy spender in reality.

Check out some of these nifty websites. They offer a lot of good information and links on how to save on basic household expenses. Remember you can find many more sites, blogs, savings and budget advice by searching for phrases such as frugal living, lower bills, save money, cut expenses, etc. Look around, ask people and see what works best for you.

www.frugalliving.about.com
www.savemoney.com
www.saylowerbills.com
www.whitefence.com

PERIODIC REVIEW

Every six months or so review your bills and check current prices for the services you use. Don't be afraid to ask for a discount from your bank, cable provider, credit card etc. If you notice a heavily discounted rate for new customers, you might want to call their customer service line and ask for that same discount.

If you pay your bill on time and have been a good customer, they may be willing to match the teaser rate to keep you from shopping around and possibly cancelling your account. Remember to tell them where and when you saw the offer, so they can verify the details. You may need to talk to a supervisor; the customer service person answering the phone may not have the authority to grant your request. The company may decline your request, but then you can go ahead and shop around.

Scrutinize your billing statements. Do you pay a monthly account processing fee? Does the company offer quarterly, semi-annual, yearly or paperless online billing options for a reduced price, fewer fees, or a one-time reward? When it comes time to renew subscriptions see if the publication offers heavy discounts for two or three year subscriptions. Find out if your health club offers discounted rates if you pay 6 months or a year at a time.

Our town's newspaper offers the lowest monthly subscription fees for customers who set up automatic payment with a credit card. Plus if you have a reward-based card you get points for each purchase, even if it is a monthly bill.

SAVVY Mom's credit card offered a $5 bonus for signing up for paperless billing via email. Hug a tree, be green, and save money too. Now that's worth celebrating with a fishy treat!

Insurance companies happily send you a monthly bill, but most charge an additional handling fee for the convenience. If the fee is $4 a month, that's $48 plus 12 first class stamps, and 12 checks used to send your payment. Go to semi-annual payments and those fees get waived. Bye, bye!

Multiply your savings using a free online

> It Pays to Check Those Bills:
> A recent review of SAVVY Family's credit card transactions, phone and other billing statements turned up close to $42 per month in charges for services rarely or never used. A few quick calls and some online account adjustments netted a savings of close to $500 per year for about two hours of time spent.

bill paying service through your bank and credit union. Some banks charge a fee for the service, but others don't. If you can find a deal use it. All those small fees reduced or eliminated, plus the unused stamps and checks add up to real money during the course of the year. You may just save a bundle.

ANNUAL BILL REVIEW/ AUDIT

Many of us operate on auto-pilot when paying monthly bills. Due to a lack of time or disinterest it seems easy to just write out a check or make a quick electronic payment. Aside from writing down the total due, the contents or details of the billing get ignored. This can be costly. When SAVVY Mom decided to follow my advice the result shocked even her. I dare say auditing those bills will likely be much more frequent in our household in 2009. See what a few changes netted us in tuna money:

PROJECTED SAVINGS OVER 2008

CATEGORY	2009 SAVINGS	
CAR INSURANCE	$100	Raised Deductible
CELL PHONE	$80	Cancelled Unused Service
CONTRIBUTION	$440	Reduced Allocation
CREDIT CARD AUDIT	$198	Unused Services
HOMEOWNERS INS.	$94	Better Rate Available
PRESCRIPTIONS	$588	Generic & Mail Order
Total	$1,500	

Source: THE SAVVY FAMILY BILLS

LOOK FOR BANKING DEALS

If you take the time to look around, banking deals abound. Just remember to confirm your account is FDIC (Federal Deposit Insurance Corporation) insured. Money Market accounts can fluctuate with Wall Street ups and downs and they are not always guaranteed by the government. Again, being savvy means asking questions and being smart. That means you talk to the bank, ask information about your accounts, ask questions about fees for various services, and confirm your deposits are covered.

Banks like to compete for business by offering cash bonuses, gift cards, IPods, GPS systems and the like. Gone are the days of the free toaster Grandma got from her banker. Also check if your bank has special rates or deals for kids or college students. SAVVY Dad recently signed up for a free checking account at a local bank because they offered a time-limited deal that gave him a $100 bonus after 12 weeks for an initial $100 deposit. Calculate that rate of return for an hour of effort. Woo Hoo…thanks to WAMU!

Scan your local newspaper for banking deals and check online for deals. I checked MSN Money and found I could select my state and city to find the best checking and credit card rates in my area. Financial websites and magazines are also a good source of this type of information. That WAMU deal was included in a weekly shopping flyer the postman drops through my door slot. SAVVY Mom always scans those ads before recycling them. Once there was a coupon for a free lotto ticket. You never know what goodies hide in the junk mail.

With a good banking and credit history you will be offered the best deals. Sound money management pays for itself. Any sacrifice you make to maintain good credit will reward you in many ways. You may qualify for a larger loan, a lower down-payment or interest rate, etc.

One place to start is www.bankrate.com. You can find other resources by searching for banking deals, bank promotions, etc.

www.bankrate.com

www.fdic.gov

DEALING WITH INSURANCE

Those outrageous, nasty insurance premiums feel like money delivered on a platinum platter to big rich conglomerates. You hope you never need it, but heaven help if you don't have it. No matter whether it is medical, dental, auto, life, liability or home coverage it seems those bills keep showing up and the premiums seem higher than ever.

I purrsonally think time moves faster in the insurance industry. I dare say their version of six months is a blink of an eye in my hood. Maybe not, but it sure feels like it every time one of the monster bills drops through the mail slot. I nearly got thwacked on the head by the last 50 page premium, statement of coverage and disclaimers dropped through the door. Luckily I managed to scoot out of the way avoiding a grievous tragedy. Of course a big purrsonal injury suit might assuage some of the pain and suffering had I been hurt.

Here are some quick ideas to make sure you are getting the biggest bang for your insurance buck.

- ✓ Rethink insurance deductibles. If you have to make a claim, how large a deductible would not break your budget? If the lowest deductible, generally $100, is as much as you can handle choose that. If you can afford to raise the deductible to $250, $500 or even $1000 or more, the cost of your coverage drops significantly.
- ✓ Review deductibles annually. As your income grows raise your deductibles.
- ✓ Insure your apartment, home, and cars with a single carrier, most offer discounts for multiple policies.
- ✓ Investigate if you qualify for special group discounts. SAVVY Dad gets discounted rates from GEICO since he is a government employee and a member of a professional engineering association.
- ✓ Take a driver education course. This is obvious for teens or new drivers, but many insurance companies offer older drivers a discount if they take refresher driving safety courses after fifty, sixty, etc. One good program 55Alive is offered by AARP (American Association of Retired Persons). Check it out at www.aarp.org.
- ✓ Drive SAVVY, avoid tickets and be safe out there.
- ✓ Good grades mean lower rates for young drivers, check if your student has a B average or better.
- ✓ Maintain a good credit rating. Insurance companies find people with good credit, tend to have fewer accidents and make fewer claims, hence good credit may lower your

insurance rate. GEICO offered SAVVY Family a 10% discount for a high credit rating. It was a big rebate since they just added a teen, male driver and a new vehicle to the mix.

✓ Use your insurance for the big stuff. Before you make any claim figure out if you would be better off just paying out- of-pocket. SAVVY Family chose not to make an insurance claim after a burglary since the loss amounted to $1000 and their deductible was $750.

Medical, vision, and dental insurance cost least if you qualify for a group plan of some sort. Remember to check if you qualify for a Flexible Spending Plan (FSA) or Health Savings Plan (HSA). The dollars you allocate to these plans to cover deductibles or other health costs, reduce your taxable income and save you money.

As insurance costs rise, more employers decide to cut coverage, switch to high deductible plans, pass on the cost by increasing co-pays and premiums, or eliminate spouse and dependent services. Worse yet, a lost job means, no coverage, or your premium skyrockets under a COBRA provision. A COBRA sounds poisonous to me. I suspect many agree once they see the monthly cost. There may be a government subsidy of the cost in the new economic stimulus plan. Look for more information on these plans at the Department of Labor, www.dol.gov. You have a limited time to make a decision regarding COBRA coverage. If you don't sign up during the 60 day enrollment period after a job loss you are out of luck. That mistake may literally cost you an arm and a leg if you delay necessary medical care.

Unfortunately, many Americans do not have access to affordable insurance. If you are one of the uninsured it takes fortitude and research to discover options that may be available to you. Some communities offer free or low cost public health clinics. Horrors, you say, I'd rather die. Go right ahead, but these clinics offer folks with no medical insurance a place to go for basic care, vaccinations, etc. without resorting to visiting the local Emergency Room.

To find resources in your community contact your local health department, United Way, or search online at the library for free or low cost medical and dental care. A web search for services in Tacoma, Washington, turned up the Community Health Program. This group offers free or low cost medical and dental care and operates its own pharmacy. If you live in this area, visit http://www.commhealth.org/ for information on services and fees.

Also check for mobile clinics that come to the neighborhoods, towns, and rural areas to serve patients on a regular basis. The local public health department, local hospitals and medical centers frequently post information about upcoming events in your area. Many communities offer children's immunization clinics in the weeks before school starts. Ask your kid's school nurse for a list of programs in your area.

CASH RULES – NEGOTIATE THE SAVVY WAY

Don't be afraid to ask for cash discounts for medical services. Shop around. Prices for medical procedures and services vary widely. If you have no insurance, a high deductible, or just want to save money, ask if you can get a better rate for cash, or a lump sum payment. Cash keeps costs down. It cuts out billing costs, fees for credit processing, and staff time to handle checks, billings, and deposits.

Doctors, hospitals, and health service providers are in business. Most of us have no problem negotiating a cash price with a car salesman, electrician, or plumber. Medical services are an area few of us even consider asking for a better price. Why not try?

Some doctors list cash prices upfront. SAVVY Mom saved $200 on the price of her boy's orthodontia by paying for the entire service upfront rather than choosing a monthly payment plan. Even if you don't have a lot of money you may be able to negotiate some sort of discount or reduced price.

Many retailers will discount your price 5-10% or more for cash payments on big ticket items too. SAVVY Dad used this technique to pay for SAVVY Mom's sparkly ruby and diamond engagement ring. That saved a couple of Ben Franklins and the additional sales tax to boot.

You may get turned down, but, again, you may just save a few bucks. As my sage spiritual advisor says, "He who meows the least pays the most." Good advice, indeed.

CUT PRESCRIPTION COSTS

Prescription costs can vary widely at different pharmacies. Shop around for the lowest price if you do not have prescription coverage. Call local pharmacies directly or check for information online at the store web sites. Costco does not require you to be a member to access their pharmacy and optometric services.

Do you have prescriptions you fill regularly? If so, check if competing pharmacies offer any deals to get you to transfer your prescription. The Target Pharmacy Rewards program offers a 10% off shopping day for every 10 prescriptions filled – it even works on prescription purchases if you time it right. In my town different pharmacies offer $20 to $30 gift cards to their stores to entice you to transfer a prescription. One place recently offered to accept up to four transferred prescriptions for a total payout of $120. If you have several pharmacies within a reasonable distance, and you don't mind switching you can take advantage of these offers.

If you do not have prescription coverage in your medical plan see if you can find a pharmacy that offers a good price plus a freebie for switching your business. Loyalty is for the birds if you can get a high value payout for your time and effort.

Go generic with your prescriptions. Generic prescriptions generally have the same quality and performance as name-brand drugs at a fraction of the cost. SAVVY Mom elected to switch to a generic medicine. That move reduced her co-pay by $15 per month or $180 a year. A number of big chains, Wal-Mart, Target, Walgreens, COSTCO and others, offer inexpensive flat-rate generic prescriptions on a long list of common generic medicines. Some offer common prescriptions for $4 a month or $10 for a 90-day supply. Recently, the Rite Aid store in our area advertised a new, free prescription club card. The plan charges $8 for generics and gives 20% off all other prescription prices. Some of these programs limit eligibility to folks with limited or no prescription drug coverage. Check with your pharmacist to see if you may qualify. If your pharmacy does not offer a discount, but another does make the switch.

If you can't afford your medicine don't suffer in silence. It pays to talk to your doctor. Sometimes your doctor can contact their pharmaceutical representative to get samples of drugs you need. Some pharmaceutical companies provide prescriptions to low-income patients without insurance coverage through their own special programs. If you qualify your doctor's office can help you fill out the forms. Also check out the Partnership for Prescription Assistance at www.pparx.org.

If you have prescription drug coverage, investigate whether or not you can use a mail-order pharmacy to get a 3 month supply of your prescription delivered to your home. Some insurers will offer a reduced co-payment for doing this, plus the medicine is delivered directly to your home saving you the time, gas and hassle of schlepping to the pharmacy monthly. SAVVY Mom recently elected this option for the family at a savings of several hundred dollars a year in co-pays alone.

When your doctor wants you to try a new prescription ask if he/she has a sample pack to use first. That way, you can take the drug for a few days before you get the prescription filled and pay your co-pay or whatever: that way if you have adverse side-effects you most likely will discover them before you plunk down money for a prescription you end up tossing.

www.pparx.org

HEALTH CARE FOR THE FURRY SET

Just a little Public Service Announcement for the furry people in your life. I'm referring to the puss, dog or other fuzzy pal, not cousin Harry the human werewolf. When money gets tight at home, routine vaccinations and essentials like spaying and neutering may get delayed or dropped altogether. Both scenarios are bad for your pet and your community.

Check with your local humane society, veterinarian, or animal shelter to find if low-cost spay/neuter clinics or pet vaccination clinics are available in your locale. In Washington State 1-877-4SpayWA offers referrals to clinics offering reduced cost sterilization services throughout the State.[10]

If you end up having to consider giving up your pet due to job loss, foreclosure, or some other difficulty please don't abandon your pet. Many communities have no-kill shelters or rescue groups that might be able to help you locate a temporary or permanent home for your pet. Some folks even advertise online on sites such as www.craigslist.com for foster families for their beloved animals. Some folks may be willing to house and love your pets for a short time if you pay for food or necessary medical care.

SAVVY Cat reminds you there are too many unwanted, unloved, and suffering animals in the world so don't get the bright idea to breed your purebred to sell the babies for quick money. A check of your local animal shelter will turn up the leftovers of that foul home business idea. Do not be part of the problem of animal overpopulation. Your furry family member deserves better.

If you get a new pet you may want to check into some of the pet health insurance plans. SAVVY Cat doesn't have one, but at my age I'm lucky to wake up from my morning nap so this type of plan isn't worth the cost. I understand these plans might be worthwhile if your fuzzy family members are young. Most veterinarians have brochures that explain plan options, benefits and costs.

DON'T GET SHOCKED BY ELECTRIC BILLS, DROWNED BY WATER CHARGES, OR, BURNED BY HEATING YOUR HOME

Check with your local utility companies to see if they have any special programs or incentives to reduce your use of water, electricity, natural gas, etc. In some areas providers may offer discounted rates for energy use at non-peak times. Other utilities offer monthly budget payment options that split your average yearly energy or heating costs into more manageable fixed monthly charges.

In my town, the local water authority included a flyer in the monthly bill, advertising a water-reducing shower head and sink aerator for the asking. I signed up online to save a stamp. Purrsonally, I think bathing in water is over-rated, but humans seem to enjoy getting wet and rubbing suds all over their bodies, so it's a nice treat for them and a savvy move for me. Let's just keep the zero, zilch, nada cost a secret from them. I like to impress them with my largesse now and again.

Also ask your utility about free energy checks. Their energy detectives can show you all the little places heat, cool air and electricity disappear and offer great suggestions to cut your loss of energy. It may lower your bill, or at least give you the facts to choose how or whether to make changes. You might even help the environment too.

Replace your old bulbs with compact fluorescent lights. SAVVY Mom found heavily discounted compact fluorescent light bulbs at the big warehouse home improvement store. Just like the free aerators, the local energy utilities worked with local companies to offer a lamp and light exchange program in our area. Again, this notice was in the billing statement that sailed through our mailbox. Skim through bill inserts to catch these offers.

Energy efficient windows keep your home warmer in the winter and cooler in the summer. Your utility might even offer a special low-interest loan or discount program. You might consider using an inexpensive, insulating adhesive film you can put on your windows yourself. The film keeps the room measurably cooler in warm weather and warmer in the cold. SAVVY Dad &Mom spent about $15 to do this on two windows in our house using scissors to cut the film and a blow dryer to seal the bond.

If you use heating oil, some companies offer a discount if you pay for the fill-up before the company bills you. A 2% discount on an $800 heating oil bill is worth $16 if you set aside the cash ahead of time. During the summer set aside some of the cash you would have spent on heat and save it for the next cold season.

Call your local Solid Waste Management Service (the garbage collector) and ask if they offer a lower fee for using a smaller capacity garbage container. When my family reduced the size of our garbage can from 60 to 20 gallons it saved us several dollars a month. We also started recycling more. Our town offers 90 gallon recycling bins and 90 gallon yard waste bins free for the asking. We manage to fill two recycling bins and one yard waste bin every two weeks. Plus the City collects the bins curbside so we save added trips to the recycler or dump. Spending less time, money and gas plus saving the planet at the same time – Go Green!!!

Creativity and flexibility hallmark frugal families. At the very least take a bit of time to see what changes you can make. Get the kids involved. Challenge each other to see who can trim energy use and cut expenses. You may find some clever solutions that save energy and money too.

This competition strategy works great with the pre-teen set. If you have tweens or teens you may find it harder to get them on board. When my family unloaded my college-age bro and his computer gear, amps, electric guitars, Xbox thingy, TV, etc. our energy bill plummeted simultaneously. Our water use dropped magically as well, now that Mr. Clean no longer showers 20 to 30 minutes twice or more a day; at least not at our address. So far our utility bill dropped about $50 per month. That adds up to about $600 a year.

With dramatic savings like that more folks may want to pawn off their teen energy sponges onto grandparents or other relatives a few months a year. Factor in the cost of food and entertainment, and this savvy move could save you a ton of money. Just make sure no one, but you know the real reason you sent them to visit for the summer.

ENERGY STAR SAVINGS

Even the US government can help you shave dollars off energy costs. Check out the great tips at www.energystar.gov. Remember you've paid for this site with your tax dollars so you may as well get some of that money back in your pocket by following the advice of these savvy bureaucrats. The feds detail numerous ways to audit your home energy use, find efficient appliances, and save money. A few minutes spent checking their advice could pay off in real cash down the road.

When you buy new appliances check their Energy Star ratings. You may even find it less expensive to replace old appliances with new more efficient models. If you decide to purchase a new appliance, or switch from oil to electricity or natural gas, do the math first. You need to calculate the cost of the change versus the potential long-term savings. If you plan on moving in a few years or know you will stay put forever, factor that in too. Energystar.gov offers over 50 categories of energy efficient products from washers and insulation to battery chargers, televisions and windows.

If you decide to replace an older appliance, check the energy ratings, take the time to compare prices, and look for any specials or outlet store bargains on the model in your area. Some stores have a clearance corner with scratch and dent items, or periodically scan the sales and pounce when the price is right. Many retailers offer rebates on delivery of large or bulky items and will sometimes haul off your old model for free.

Energy Star sponsors a cool educational website just for children. Entertain your rug rats for free. That might keep them occupied long enough for kitty to get some shut eye. Your puss will thank you, plus the kids just might forgive you the next time you holler at them for forgetting to turn off the lights when they leave a room.

www.energystar.gov

KEEP WARRANTIES HANDY

Keep important instruction manuals and warranty information together in a file. Attach the sale's receipt and promptly mail in any warranty registration cards. Most companies offer a postage paid card or envelope for this purpose, so it should cost you nothing to record your purchase and validate the product warranty.

Many warranty periods range from 30 days to several years. In the case of vehicles, it typically includes a number of years or a specific mileage benchmark. You may also receive additional warranty protection if you purchase an item with a major credit card. Check your card's contract.

Your warranty file saves loads of time and effort when something important goes haywire. This is

ARE EXTENDED WARRANTIES SAVVY?

Deciding if you should to purchase a retailer's extended-warranty plan can be tough. SAVVY Cat rarely springs extra for this option unless the item it covers is high tech and expensive to repair or replace.

SAVVY Mom chose to pay for three years onsite repair/replacement for the laptop she relies on to transcribe my important thoughts. One cup of coffee spilled on the keyboard, one clumsy trip on a power cord, or a tragic hard-drive crash and the $300 charge pays for itself.

Of course, regular back-ups of important files, gives me peace of mind that my profound advice will not be lost in a cyber blowout, blackout, or some other random electronic tragedy.

especially true for cars. For some strange reason, our family's vehicles suffer an inordinate rate of transmission failures. Despite SAVVY Mom's best consumer research several relatively new transmissions died in three different makes and models of our cars. All repairs, except one were covered under warranties. Let's just hope the jinx ends.

Do not hesitate to use warranties. In some cases companies will repair or replace your merchandise at no charge. Contact the manufacturer's customer service center by phone or online for specific instructions. Some companies will mail you appropriate packaging materials and pre-paid postage. Follow all instructions, enclose copies of pertinent receipts, write a description of the problem, then wait. In some cases you may have to take your item to a local authorized warranty repair facility.

Be sure to follow-up with the repair facility or company if necessary, especially if the wait drags on from weeks into months. SAVVY Mom waited patiently for six months for a replacement crank for her fancy recumbent exercise bike. When she finally called, the company admitted they couldn't locate the part so they sent a replacement bicycle. Of course we have to deal with the dead bike carcass in the basement, but Mom is back to riding up and down imaginary hills while she reads or watches TV.

Even if you think the warranty may be expired call the customer service line and check it out. Sometimes manufacturers will extend coverage or locate replacement parts even when your item is off warranty. It pays to ask and most businesses offer a toll-free line or can be contacted online via email at no cost to you.

BUNDLE UP

Bundle up grandma used to say, or you will catch your death of cold. Today, bundle up means something entirely different from putting on a big, cozy sweater. Bundling up can be key to getting the best rates for a package of services.

Cellular and phone companies combine services like long-distance minutes, caller ID, call waiting, texting, and so on. Cable and Internet providers offer bundling deals too. Some companies offer phone, internet and cable for one fee. That has to be the ultimate snuggly bundle up plan or so they would like you to think.

Be smart about making a switch. You may save what seems like big bucks over separate service plans, but ask some key questions first. Many companies offer great teaser deals for the first 6 months or so. Don't get snookered into a contract without understanding if there will be a big jump in price down the line. Also factor in deposits you may be required to pay if you are a new customer with no credit history, or have bad credit.

Again the key is talk. I thought about calling this book, *Yap Your Way to Savings*, but that sounded too much like Dr. Chihuahua wrote it, rather than *moi*.

Check online for bundling deals in your area. Talk to your current providers and see what plans they offer. If you must reduce costs fast due to a job loss or other financial emergency, you may need to keep only the most basic phone plan and drop cable and internet altogether.

Negotiate with service providers if you have a contract. They might be willing to reduce your service and the price in order to keep your account current. It costs them a lot less to work with you and keep the checks coming in, than to try and collect on bad debt. In tough economic times everyone wants to keep paying customers, even at a discount.

www.thesavvycat.com

SAVVY Mom recently spent 30 minutes or so reviewing SAVVY Family's phone, TV and internet fees. She checked prices for Tacoma at www.whitefence.com and the service provider's sites.

Our current phone service could be called a mini-bundle: a land-line phone with unlimited local and long distance, plus three premium services. With taxes and fees the package costs approximately $53 per month. No surprise bills no matter how many hours SAVVY Mom chats on the phone. A comparable long-distance service with another name brand company costs close to $15 more per month for fewer options and no local access.

SAVVY Mom and Dad use pay-as-you-go cell phones for trips, emergencies on the road, and brief calls away from home. Both phones cost about $15 each to purchase on sale and last through a number of years of use. These plans have no contract period and the net cost, excluding the purchase price of the phones comes to $21 per month for both. The per-minute rates vary depending on call length and frequency.

The bottom line: $74 per month for one land line, two cell phones plus unlimited local and long distance calling. Fortunately, the bro pays for his ultra expensive cellular phone and plan or I would be an orphan with both SAVVY Mom and Dad sharing cell bars of another sort.

Our local hi-speed cable internet and standard cable TV packages likewise remain the lowest available in their class. They meet our needs and do not require service contracts. Both are affiliated with the local public utility. Since we only have a month-to-month contracts we can change our service at any time without penalty.

The bottom line: $80 per month for cable TV for three televisions, plus cable internet and wireless for one desktop and one laptop computer. We could cut this cost more if necessary by dropping from standard to basic cable, and dropping all but one of our TV cable converter boxes, but at this time we choose to keep those perks.

Our internet provider offers cable TV and VoIP (Voice over Internet Phone) for a flat rate. Their six month teaser rate is about $30+ a month less than what we currently pay for separate phone, cable and internet services. However, after the initial teaser period, typically 6 to 12 months, that margin of savings drops considerably, plus the companies require a long-term contract versus the month-to-month plan we have now.

A number of companies offer low cost VoIP plans, or if you choose to use just cellular and drop the traditional land line, check into the method your provider uses to access 911 in emergencies. Unlike standard land-lines, VoIP and cellular plans may not automatically provide emergency services with your home address. This can mean confusion or delays in an emergency.

Be certain to question your provider about this. If they offer "Enhanced 911 Service" that means the company provides local emergency dispatch services with the customer's home address and contact information. If you move but keep the same phone service you need to confirm your emergency information gets updated too. During your annual bill review, add a call to your local non-emergency number to confirm your home address and phone number are listed correctly on the Emergency dispatcher's database

My family does not bundle services for this reason. My cross-species bro and I were home alone one morning when two robbers broke down the kitchen door. I slithered under a bed and hid with the dust bunnies. The bro exited the basement in nothing but boxers and a t-shirt. Good thing he skipped the usual marathon shower that a.m. The police arrived quickly because 911 pinpointed our home right away. We choose not to mess with what works for us because we are SAVVY CATS. A deal may not be a deal for you for purrsonal rather than financial reasons.

HOT SOLUTIONS FOR TROUBLESOME CONTRACTS

Long contracts for cellular service or car leases can seem like a jail sentence when money gets tight. Breaking a service contract usually costs an arm and a leg. If you must get out of an expensive contract try to renegotiate the terms first. Who knows? You may get lucky.

Of course if the charm tactic fails, you need to do some research and think creatively to get out of contract purgatory penalty free. Misery loves company so look online for others in your predicament. Open your internet browser and search for the phrase, "get out of cell contract free," or "get out of car lease free." You will likely find all sorts of advice (some legitimate and some not).

Another trendy place to search is www.craigslist.org. Select your location and type in cellular contract or car lease in the search box. You can see what people are offering, etc. Some companies will allow you to transfer or assume a contract or lease just make sure you follow the terms listed in your plan. The process may include a credit check, deposits etc. Just be sure to deal with a legitimate company.

Your best bet is to deal locally. If a car is involved remember to factor in transportation costs if you decide to make a deal outside of your city. Be smart: meet strangers in public places, and if a deal sounds too good to be true you may get scammed.

If you are on the dumping end, take care of the transfer paperwork and confirm you are no longer the responsible party before you let go of the goods. Some trusting folks get burned by forgetting to confirm everything is done correctly. Take the time to do it right. SAVVY Cat heard a news story about car dealerships accepting cars as trade-in, selling them and then failing to pay off previous loans as agreed. No one was the wiser until the loan company repossessed the vehicles for non-payment. That old saying "penny wise and pound foolish" applies to modern times too.

www.craigslist.org
www.leasetrader.com

CUT YOUR GROCERY BILLS

In many families the impact of rising food prices takes a toll both economically and emotionally. The weekly food budget usually gets nailed first when folks try to allocate available cash between fixed costs like rent, car payments, insurance, and variable necessities gas, power, emergency repairs, etc.

If you are like most people, you may choose to do without certain items or expenditures, you may dip into savings, you may resort to using credit, or you may tap into funds reserved for retirement, emergencies or future college expenses. The first option may work for the short term, and dipping into savings might help until you run out of cash, but turning to credit and depleting long-term retirement or college accounts will impact you for years to come.

SAVVY Mom uses a variety of strategies to spend smarter when she's picking up kibble, fish and other necessities. If you can creatively lower the cost of feeding your family, that may free up a bit of cash to help cover other rising expenses, or at least help reduce the gap between income and outgo each month. If you shave just $5 off the cost of one grocery trip, you save $5 you can spend somewhere else, or not spend at all.

If you recycle the sales insert from your Sunday paper, or if you don't subscribe to the paper you can still find deals at your favorite store each week. Go online to the store's website and look for a link to their weekly sales advertisement. Many stores have their ad links near the top of their webpage. Or just look for the stack of sales ads every store places near their doors and customer service counters.

Most grocery items go on sale in cycles. If you remain flexible you can plan meals with sale items. If you have the space and a bit of extra cash, you can stock up on items when they are on sale and add them to your larder. Recently our local **Safeway** had a deal on a premium name-brand soup, buy two get three free. That brought the cost per can down to a dollar. Time to stock up!

Some websites can help you find and sort the deals at your local stores. You can do this yourself using the advertising inserts in your local paper, but if you shop at some of the major regional grocery chains free online services find the deals at your local store each week. The site, www.mygrocerydeals.com sorts specials by store and allows you to create and print a grocery list. They offer free registration, coupons, and other services in over 500 cities nationwide. Other sites offer similar services for a fee. Why pay for something you can access free?

The beauty of this website is that you can customize it to your favorite local stores. They will even send email alerts when weekly sales get posted. Do you think they would come clean my purrsonal office too?

Use the site to plan your weekly meals and build your menu based on specials. You will be able to serve your family a variety of meals that are economical, healthy and within your budget. If you focus on purchasing fruits and vegetables that are in season you can get the biggest bang for your food dollars.

If you live in a city with multiple grocers close by, and you have the time, shop the sales at several stores. Feed the family on loss leaders (the sale items stores discount heavily to get you through the door).

Using coupons for sale items can save even more. The key here is flexibility and creativity. If you have freezer or storage space, and the extra cash, stock up on the cheapest deals. I could care less, but SAVVY Mom keeps stacks of TP in the basement, along with sponges, cleaning supplies, printer paper, detergent and soap.

Last week one local store had a three day fish sale. SAVVY Mom raced over to get a 7 pound salmon for $3.99/lb. She asked the fish monger to fillet the fish, which she did for free. We ended up with two large fillets one to grill, and the other triple wrapped in the freezer for another BBQ. The net cost came to $4.50 per pound for the fillets, or less than half the regular per pound sale price for a single pre-cut fillet.

If you have a sharp boning knife you can purchase a whole chicken and cut it up yourself. The savings per pound can amount to 50% or more. Cheaper cuts of meat can be marinated or slow cooked to fork cut tenderness with very little effort. SAVVY Mom loves to beat round steak into submission with a mallet before cooking to break down tough fibers. It's a great stress reliever too! I duck under the counter in case the top of the mallet flies off in my direction.

Look around your house and scout out available storage space for your SAVVY Deals. You can always store non-perishables under beds, in closets, drawers, in the garage or other places in your home. You might want to make of note of where you stash the goodies in order to keep track of what you have.

www.mygrocerydeals.com

EAT THE SPECIALS

SAVVY Mom put the following sample grocery list together using specials listed on mygrocerydeals.com. This sample list doesn't include some staple items such as flour, sugar, etc. which most folks already have on hand. The sample includes a variety of items that can be mixed and matched for breakfast, lunch and dinner menus. Of course the ten tins of tuna on the shopping list are for me.

Try to shop without hubby or kids tagging along if possible. Stick to a list and don't be swayed by pretty displays or impulse buys. If you have to shop with the kids or hubby give them a job to occupy them. Let them check items off the list, use a calculator to add items up, etc. Little kids can push the cart or be in charge of getting the boxes or cans off the shelf as you point to them. The important point is to stick as closely as possible to your list and your budget. If you can fit in a treat, perhaps you can save that for the end and the whole lot, kids and Dad, will think you are the greatest Mom on the planet.

Look for new recipes to try. Go to the library and check out recipe books, kid cooking tips, or frugal food advice. Look online for frugal recipes, cheap eating, healthy inexpensive meals, etc. You may even find a free or inexpensive class or workshop through your park district or community center. Have the kids talk to older relatives and ask them for special recipes they used to stretch their budget years ago.

You'll enjoy a good visit and get to try some new recipes that may become family favorites once again. It's also a good history lesson. Remember mock apple pie? You may uncover some interesting mystery meat recipes too. How about dandelion green salad? Have you seen the price of those babies in the upscale supermarkets lately? Grandma would have choked on her dentures if she saw how much green those so-called weeds cost today.

SAMPLE SHOPPING LIST

www.mygrocerydeals.com, 8/05/08
Shopping List Total: $92.52
FRED MEYER

2	Store Brand Hoagie Rolls (4 ea)	$3.00
1	Bandon's Medium Cheddar Cheese (2 lb)	$4.99
1	Onions (1 lb)	$0.99
3	Health Valley Chili (15 oz.)	$5.00
1	Florida's Natural Orange Juice (64oz.)	$2.99
10	Bumble Bee Tuna in Water (6 oz)	$10.00
1	Hunts Spaghetti Sauce (26 oz)	$0.79
1	Keebler Cookies (16oz)	$1.84
1	Boneless Skinless Chicken Breasts (1 lb)	$2.00

SAFEWAY

2	O Organics Organic Mini Peeled Carrots (16 oz)	$4.00
2	Fresh Express Riviera Salad Blend (7 oz)	$4.00
4	Golden Grain Elbow (12 oz)	$5.00
1	Mott's Apple Juice (64 oz)	$1.99
1	Johnsonville Original Bratwurst (19.76 oz)	$3.99
1	O Organics Organic Fat Free Milk (64 oz)	$3.29

TOP FOOD & DRUG

5	Cucumbers Organic	$3.00
1	Tomatoes Vine Ripe, Regular (1 lb)	$1.49
1	Potato Red (1 lb)	$0.79
1	Potato Yellow (1 lb)	$0.79
1	Celery Heart (1 lb)	$0.79
1	Pork Shoulder Steak (1 lb)	$1.99
1	Chicken Cut up Fryer (1 lb)	$1.49

1	Cauliflower (1 ea)	$0.89
1	Beef - Other Cuts Extra Lean Ground (1 lb)	$2.99
1	Jif Peanut Butter (28 oz)	$3.99
1	Melon Watermelon (1 ea)	$2.99
1	Melon Cantaloupe/Muskmelon (1 ea)	$0.79
1	Grapes Green Seedless (1 lb)	$1.99
1	Wheat Bread (24 oz)	$1.99
1	Pillsbury Cake Mix (18.25 oz)	$0.89
1	Greens Collard (1 lb)	$0.79
1	Steak Round (1 lb)	$2.99

Plus: Eggs, Rice, Margarine, & Cereal - $11.00 EST

DISCOUNT MEAT, PRODUCE, OR BREAD DEALS

Stores that deal in fresh perishable foods offer discounts on meat, dairy products, or other items on, or close to, pull dates. These foods are safe to eat provided they are used promptly or frozen right away. The marked down products disappear quickly so check regularly.

My neighborhood Safeway dedicates a small section of the meat case to discounted beef, pork, poultry, and fish. The packages are clearly marked with their pull date, but the butcher puts a bright sticker on the pack offering 30% 50% off the original price.

Don't be shy about asking store employees about what time of day they mark these items down. If you can schedule your shopping around these times you can maximize the selection available. Remember, you're SAVVY, not CHEAP.

Scout out the deals in your store. A local green grocer typically puts large bags of slightly distressed produce at the end of each checkout for priced at a dollar or two. The grab bags might even offer sampling of veggies and fruits. These make great additions to soups, sauces, or pasta.

Many towns have discount bakery outlets. Here you can purchase bread and other baked goods. If you have room in the freezer great, if not stop by when you are in the area on other errands, or arrange with a friend to pick up an item or two for you if they are shopping.

Again, being SAVVY is really about communication. Talk to relatives, friends, and neighbors. If you combine forces you might be able to take advantage of bulk deals or specials that you can split. If you plan on visiting the local grocery outlet or discount store ask a friend or neighbor if you can grab something for them too. When they reciprocate you might hear about an incredible deal you would have previously missed. You could even start a savings club at work, church, or school.

BE PREPARED

No one is immune from disaster, whether natural or man-made. Being prepared for emergencies, or a nation-wide kibble rationing crisis, requires Boy Scout style commitment and planning. The government recommends 3 days supply of food and water at all times. FEMA (the Federal Emergency Management Administration), www.fema.gov, offers some great planning tools, lists, and advice. They even have a fun educational website for kids chock full of disaster facts, pictures, games, and other cool info about how to prepare for emergencies.

No need to buy expensive kits, just make a conscious effort to set aside a few things here and there. You can use a large plastic tote or box to store your survival stockpile. If you buy a case of water take a few bottles and add them to the kit, grab a roll of toilet paper, put in a couple of easy-open cans of fruit, beans, tuna, spam, etc. Add soap, hand sanitizer, and other items as you get freebies, samples, or other items on sale. Build your kit a bit at time, and the cost won't break the bank.

I purrsonally like to hoard bottled water, easy-open tuna tins, kibble, litter, toilet paper, hand-sanitizer, duct tape, tarps and coffee. The first few for obvious reasons the others for speculative reasons; you can imagine what water, TP, tarps and duct tape will fetch on the street in a crisis, let alone a cup of Joe. Add chocolate to the mix and stock up when those items go on sale, and you'll make a fortune the next time Mother Nature comes calling. I like to think of it as my purrsonal emergency hedge fund.

www.fema.gov

PANTRY INVENTORY & MINI-SHOP WEEK

Keep track of the items you have in your home pantry. Using pantry items creatively can shave dollars off your weekly grocery tab. As you plan meals incorporate stored items into your weekly menu.

SAVVY Mom organizes the pantry food with the earliest pull dates up front. Each week, items with close expiration dates get added to the menu. This ensures food gets used when it tastes best and contains the most nutrients.

Throughout the year, you can declare a no spend week and eat through your pantry. Plan only on purchasing milk, eggs, and other fresh perishables you need to supplement your stash. Some folks do this for two weeks or a month, but that takes real commitment and a significant stockpile of food.

If you cut $50 off your grocery bill during that week you can use the dollars you save to pay down an outstanding bill, or for savings or family fun. View it as an adventure or family challenge and work together as a team. You might even come up with some innovative, savvy recipes for the latest best selling kid's cookbook. At the very least you'll enjoy cooking together and learning to create healthful, inexpensive meals. Woo Hoo!!!

BROWN BAGGING IS CHIC

Cutting down on lunches out can free up oodles of extra cash. Just think if you typically spend a mere $5 a day for lunch that equals $25 a week, or $100 a month. Add a $3 snack or coffee drink to that and your work day tally adds up to over $1700 a year or more.

Brown bagging at least four days a week saves a bundle. Add no fancy coffee or snacks for four days a week and the total grows. SAVVY Dad likes to eat a modest lunch out each Friday. He enjoys anticipating whether it will be Pakistani, Japanese, Vietnamese or Thai. Living in the Puget Sound region really opens up the possibilities.

The brown bag sandwich routine is hotter than hot right now. Mosey on down to the company lunchroom and you will likely find only a few empty seats in a room that previously collected little more than dirty coffee mugs and dust.

Guys, eat your lunch at the local park when the weather is sunny. It's a great way to meet the babes. Gals love to picnic plus they will think you are one cool alfresco lunching dude. Just watch out for the flying bird bombs when you dine outdoors. Also, remember to be a good visitor and pack out your garbage.

Better yet, turn lunch into a party! Get your co-workers interested in a frugal potluck. Limit everyone to a $3 contribution of some sort. One person buys shredded cheese, another buys tortillas, another refried beans and combine the goodies and nuke some burritos. Others can contribute $3 worth of shredded lettuce, diced veggies, sliced olives, or other stuff. Let your imagination roll.

I dare say you will save a bit of moola, encourage a sense of community, and likely learn some interesting purrsonal facts about your co-workers. Make this a frugal competition. Have everyone present their receipts and crown the savviest shopper with a paper hat. You may even impress your boss with your spectacular financial acumen. That next promotion just might be yours.

You could even try this event at home or with friends. Or try a progressive dinner party- snacks at one place, salad at another, a BBQ at a third, and finally dessert at the end. If there is drinking involved, designate a driver to take revelers from place to place.

Your kids might enjoy planning lunches or meals within a budget. If money motivates your kids offer them a percentage of the money saved by brown-bagging lunches or skipping take-out. Replace money worries with a new sense of adventure in dining. Bon Appétit!!!

MAXIMIZE SAVINGS WITH COUPONS & SALES

I find coupons everywhere, even under my litter box. They come in the mail, in the newspaper, lie in wait in the grocery aisles, and hide online. With a little effort you can shave loads off the cost of everyday items and special goodies and treats.

I love the Sunday paper I find it purrfect for testing the shredding power of newly sharpened claws. The enormous size presents many opportunities for pointed assessment. That's a little cat humor for my feline buddies. MEOW DUDES!!! The second biggest weekly paper comes out on Wednesday, stuffed with all the glorious grocery ads for tuna, salmon, and mackerel sales.

My humans love those same papers, but for different reasons. The Sunday paper contains special inserts I rarely get to shred. These mysterious papers are worth money. *Ipso facto* my caretakers don't allow me too close to them. These inserts contain manufacturer's coupons.

I've noticed you practically need a forklift to hoist those Sunday and Wednesday papers onto the couch for reading. Colorful advertising inserts generally make up 90% of paper. Combine the sales in those pretty inserts with the slips of clipped coupon paper and shave even more off the price of kibble at the market. Each Sunday, my translator separates these inserts from the bad news of the day and saves them for later scrutiny.

The coupons, offers, and refunds included within those pages equal the value of paper from the US Mint. They represent free money, cold hard cash; a quarter, half-dollar, a dollar or more off products you use or may want to try. On especially good days, inserts include coupons or rebates for free products such as the latest flavor of kibble, the newest bathroom cleanser, or a free bag of pine kitty litter.

Sometimes they offer goodies for canines too, but I really could care less. However, SAVVY Mom redeems doggy freebies to give to my cousin Zobe Dog. We also sometimes give them to the local animal shelter.

The big bonus of this free moola is that the U.S. government does not consider this income. In one year my family's accumulated coupon savings added up to more than $1000 tax free. That is more like $1300 free if you consider our tax bracket. Don't dismiss clipping coupons as too much trouble to manage. Who couldn't use an extra grand or more TAX FREE each year? Of course if you are so rich you don't need any free cash, you can ignore this tip.

If you would like to use coupons on your favorite products and don't like to clip them you can investigate a coupon clipping service. SAVVY Mom found one online site, www.thecouponclippers.com by searching for coupon clipping services through her favorite search engine. Other clipping services abound so look around. Most sites allow you to browse their inventory so you can see if they have coupons you would use. Remember to read the description carefully and check expiration dates. There is no sense ordering coupons that expire before you can redeem them. You may be asked to purchase a minimum amount too. These sites generally require you to register and you pay a small clipping and mailing fee.

If you find higher value coupons for specific products you use regularly, the service may be worth trying. Most sites require you pay with a credit card or, but a debit card with a VISA or MASTERCARD logo also works. Another alternative is to set up a PayPal account at www.paypal.com and transfer funds electronically. Your coupons usually arrive in a few days.

SAVVY Mom placed a test order with thecouponclippers.com on a Thursday. She selected coupons for sale items listed in that week's store flyer. The coupons arrived the following Monday. She finished the weekly shopping on Tuesday (in our area grocery stores ads run Wed. through Tues.) paying $113.20 for $234.00 worth of items. The discounts included reward card savings, bonus savings for purchasing particular items in certain quantities, plus $22+ in paper coupons.

Some stores offer to double or even triple manufacturer's coupons up to a set limit. One local store sometimes includes four double coupon certificates with a maximum value of $1, which means the store matches a coupon up to $1 in value. That's $2 off! Check it out, you may find you live in coupon nirvana.

Electronic coupons are all the rage these days. Some retailers link their store reward/loyalty cards to online coupon services. When you check out, the coupons get deducted automatically. Go to www.shortcuts.com/stores, search for your zip code and check if there are any participating stores in your area. Go green, save money, save trees, now that is a real deal.

Speaking of E-coupons, the college savings site www.UPromise.com (See You Promise What?) just started offering grocery coupons as one of their many savings options. They link the selected coupons to your supermarket loyalty card. Imagine getting cents off groceries, cents for college, it makes good sense even to me.

SAVVY CATS stack as many savings as possible into to each and every purchase. Bit by bit the rewards accumulate. You and yours will be high-fiving the joy of the hunt and the thrill of saving money every which way.

www.shortcuts.com
www.thecouponclippers.com

TAKE ADVANTAGE OF STORE REWARD PROGRAMS

Special Web Promotions
Many national retailers offer specials online you can use locally. These offers can be found on the homepage of the store's website. Look for banners, frequently at the top, bottom, or sides of the page, that offer printable coupons, email only promotions, etc. If you don't see any use the site's search box, which is usually located near the top of the page and type in phrases such as: promotions, coupons, specials and rebates. Another option is to use your web browser to search for the store's name plus words such as online deals, coupons, or promotions.

In my hood Albertsons, Safeway, Rite Aid, Office Depot, Fred Meyer, OfficeMax and other retailers give reward memberships to shoppers for free. The premiums offered can vary from a special club member only sales price, bonus coupons or cash toward another shopping trip, discounts on gasoline, to airline miles, movie tickets, gift cards, etc. SAVVY Mom recently received emails from www.jcpenney.com and www.eddiebauer.com introducing new loyalty s programs they initiated.

Fred Meyer sponsors a bonus/rebate program based on quarterly purchases. In addition to their regular club card offers Safeway gives a fuel discount based on 10 cents per gallon for each $100 spent at the store. The last fill-up for the Catmobile netted a 40 cent/gallon discount. Safeway also offers online shopping and frequently emails codes for free delivery with a minimum order. The Post Office gets into the act delivering reward coupons via snail-mail to card holders too.

By chance we discovered the local Rite Aid discounts an additional 20% or more off regularly-priced merchandise purchased on the first Tuesday of the month. On the remaining Tuesdays of the month they offer a discount around 10%. These do not apply to alcoholic beverages, tobacco, or prescriptions. Combine this discount with their regular sales, coupons, rebates, etc. Pay with a credit card that gives you points and voila you can shave a big chunk off your bill. You need to register for one of their little reward cards, but go for it.

Rite Aid also allows you to submit rebate information online. SAVVY Mom shops for Rite Aid Rebate Rewards and a manufacturer's rebate for another product. She submits the store rebate information online, and then mails the manufacturer's rebate with the original store receipt and proof of purchase. Double-dipping freebies; what a savvy deal!!!

Walgreens adds 10% to your rebate total if you select to receive your rebate as a reusable gift card instead of a check. Walgreens started accepting online rebate submission in some markets too.

You will also find that many stores will allow you to use a manufacturer's coupon along with their store coupon. For example, if Walgreens has Tidy Cat for $1.99 with their own store coupon, you can combine a manufacturer's cents-off coupon with the Walgreens coupon, for double savings. Look at the top of your coupon next to the expiration date, store coupons have the store name rather than the generic *Manufacturer's Coupon.*

Sign up online to receive emails from the stores you frequent. Walgreens sometimes sends coupons for $5 off a $20 purchase that can be printed and used in their brick and mortar stores. Brick and mortar, that's cyber speak for a real building. Sears sent two $5 gift cards for signing up for their email ads. K-Mart offers a similar deal on their website.

Target Pharmacy Rewards sends a coupon for 10% off one day of shopping with every 10 prescriptions purchased with their Visa card. SAVVY Mom combines that reward with manufacturer's coupons, rebates and advertised specials to stock up on household supplies. Check the expiration date on the reward coupon; if you plan your shopping trip to coincide with when you pick up monthly prescriptions you get 10% off their price too. The Target Visa also sends a 10% discount shopping coupon when your cumulative spending on the card reaches $1000. Just be sure to pay the card off in full each month.

Learn where stores place special deals and clearance items. The neighborhood Safeway and Walgreens place clearance items in carts located near the front of the store. Target generally places special sale and clearance merchandise on the end caps of the aisles. Check their weekly ad for sale or bonus-size products they promote by offering a free $5 gift card with a specific purchase. SAVVY Mom netted three free $5 Target gift cards by stocking up on sale-priced coffee. If you have a Super Target store that includes groceries check the prices on products you use, some beat the grocery store.

Many major credit cards offer reward programs and other promotions. One holiday American Express promoted a $25 rebate on the purchase of $100 worth of gift cards. The net profit after a service fee was $19, almost 20%. Some retail and restaurant chains offer similar gift card promotions during the holiday season. Look for signs at

www.thesavvycat.com

check out stands, in newspapers, websites or flyers posted on the doors or windows of the establishment.

Some folks prefer not to join reward programs regardless of the deals. One friend doesn't like the feeling that someone can track his shopping habits. That's ok. You know your comfort level with reward cards, online shopping, and the like. Do what works for your family.

LOOK LOCALLY FOR SAVINGS

Many local restaurants, coffee shops, and stores offer some sort of loyalty program as well. Others send coupons, discounts or special deals via snail mail, or in shopping inserts. Look through the junk mail you get in your mailbox before tossing it in the recycling bin. Just today, a local restaurant sent a $20 gift card to entice us to visit in the next month. Mummy's birthday is coming up and that little freebie might be the purrfect gift from me.

Look up your favorite restaurant's website and see if they offer coupons, discounts or specials online. Some will even let you register birthdays or anniversaries so they can send coupons for a free appetizer, desert or dinner.

Caffeine junkies can probably find a local shop that offers the 10th cup free. I save punch cards for coffee, pizza, sandwiches, teriyaki, thrift stores and more. I keep my good as gold treasures handy and dutifully present them with applicable purchases.

It may take weeks or months to get a freebie, but wow! Nothing beats free teriyaki chicken on my plate for dinner. High fives all around!

www.valpak.com
www.shoplocal.com

CHEAP FUN ABOUT TOWN

Free or low cost activities abound in many communities. No need to spend much more than the amount to pack a lunch or snack and walk, bike, ride the bus, or drive to check out the sights around town. In SAVVY Cat's hood the local newspaper publishes a quarterly calendar detailing free festivals and events. Many communities offer free art walks, museum days and other goodies each month.

Weekend festivals and farmer's markets happen almost every month of the year. Even if you do not spend money you will frequently find these events offer free admission, music, interesting products, and low-cost or free children's activities. This last summer one local festival in Tacoma let kids help paint a mural in the middle of the street. Of course, the street was blocked off so the kiddies didn't have to dodge traffic to join in the fun.

Look for notices in the newspaper, flyers at the library or school and check out online freebies by searching for free events in your town. Your local park district may offer classes or events for school children. In Tacoma, the park service offers activities and free lunches to kids during the summer at certain parks. They also sponsor movies in the park after dark in the warmer months

When SAVVY Bro was younger the local skate-o-rama let parents skate free Sunday afternoons. Admission and skate rental was less than $5 for the three of us. Add another $5 for cheap snacks and we had one sweet, cheapskate deal. Plus we got to learn to do the Macarena and the Hokey Pokey on wheels!

Take advantage of these offers and enjoy family time on the cheap. Or just go to the park and play with your kids. SAVVY Mom and Dad played on the slides and swings when SAVVY Bro was young. Plus it's good exercise and helps kids get their daily dose of Vitamin D, the sunshine vitamin.

CUT COSTS ONLINE

The internet offers SAVVY CATS many opportunities for great deals. A little bit of research and the creative use of coupons, discounts, reward cards and shopping rebate sites save you money and gas running around. You can even find out where to get the lowest price on many consumer goods.

You can also use a search engine to look for deals on specific items. Even if you don't purchase an item online you can research the general price for bigger ticket price items you want to buy. Plus you can check the latest deals, rebates, and coupons available.

For example, when SAVVY Mom needed a new stove she checked out prices online for Sears, Loews, Home Depot, and Best Buy. Their websites allowed her to read about the price, size, features and local availability of stoves without having to drive around town to half a dozen different stores. We eventually purchased a stove from Best Buy. To save delivery fees we ordered it online and picked it up at the store.

FREE EMAIL ACCOUNTS

If you don't want a bunch of spam loading your email inbox you can set up a free email account for your commercial goodies. Or if you don't have internet access at home, or you share a computer with someone else, you may want to consider setting up a free email account online: MSN offers Hotmail and Live.com; Google has Gmail; Yahoo sponsors Ymail and Rocketmail. Take a look at several and choose one you like. These are all easy to access from home, the office or the library. Plus it takes just a few minutes to sign up.

Open your internet browser, type in your preferred site in the search box. Once you get to the website click on the email link and follow the instructions to sign up or log on. You can usually locate the links near the top or side of the browser's home page. You will need to think of an email moniker and create a password. Your email name can be something obvious such as drcatman@xxx.com or anonymous 123abc@xxx.com.

My advice is to write down your email identity and password. They are generally case sensitive, which means if you use caps always use caps, etc. Some sites may require you use a combination of upper and lower case letters and at least one symbol or number. The more complex your username and password, the more secure your account. Anyway, the service will tell you if the name you select is available or if the password your chose is acceptable.

Open two accounts with different names and passwords. That way you can choose to use one for cyber offers, shopping, etc. and the other for correspondence with friends and family. This just keeps things organized. If you don't want to take time to sort through spam or deal mail you can just open your purrsonal email account and read the latest note from dear Auntie Em.

Remember if you do this at work make sure this is an acceptable use of your office equipment. Some folks forget the IT head can read email correspondence and track internet use on the company server. Don't get yourself in hot water with the boss if cyber-surfing is restricted or banned at work. I dare say if more folks used the Grandma Rule to vet the sites they surfed there would be far fewer problems in the workplace. The Grandma Rule means that you don't look at, or access websites Grandma would be shocked to see. Of course if Gramma was one of the original Hell's Angels' biker gals you may have a wider leeway.

SOME SITES THE SAVVY CAT SURFS

Price Comparison:
www.bizrate.com
www.pricegrabber.com
www.pricescan.com
www.shopzilla.com

Online, Deals & Promotions:
www.dealhunting.com
www.entertainment.com
www.eversave.com
www.savings_center.com
www.slickdeals.net

Coupons, Samples & Savings:
www.coupons.com
www.mysavings.com
www.smartsource.com
www.valpak.com

Rewards:
www.fatwallet.com
www.mypoints.com
www.upromise.com

This list shows a sample of the many places to find deals. Check out different sites and find one that suits your needs. Most let you register free. Beware of sites that require dues or a monthly subscription. When you click a link at one of these sites, then make a purchase at a big-name retailer, it is likely your purchase benefits them through some sort of affiliate program. Many retailers offer a bounty amounting to a small percentage of each sale made through links from affiliate websites. It's safe to shop through these links, just be savvy about how people make money off the web. Rebate and reward sites give you a percentage back in the form of cash or points.

Bottom Covers Packing Slip		
6 Pair Pink Panties – Granny Style Clearance		$1.85
	WA Sales Tax	$0.14
FREESHIP2	USPS Parcel	$0 00
	TOTAL:	$1.99

Regularity is a good thing. I like to check some sites such as Slick Deals and Deal Hunting on a regular basis. One day there was a clearance sale and coupon deal at a well-known online undies store, I scored a six-pack of granny panties for Mummy for less than $2 shipped. I dare say her buns look a lot prettier in pink these days.

Many of these sites also offer printable grocery coupons. Check with your local retailer first to see if they accept internet coupons printed at home. Unfortunately, some people take advantage of these online offers and print more than the amount allowed. These folks use the coupons to clean out store shelves when an item goes on sale. This is fraud. Some stores stop accepting all printed coupons as a result. This type of behavior ruins the deal for the rest of us.

In my area Rite Aid does not accept these coupons, and some Safeway stores no longer accept them. I also noticed that my local Target posted a notice they will no longer honor certain ones as well. So ask your favorite retailer before you waste expensive printer ink and paper on what may be a worthless piece of paper.

MISERY LOVES COMPANY JOIN A GROUP

Misery loves company or so the saying goes. You can find loads of inspiration online reading blogs or checking out message boards dealing with finance, money, saving, frugal living, etc. Read through the discussions and pick up tips, inspiration, or feel a bit self-righteous. SAVVY Mom likes to check out the community boards on MSN Money and read about the latest trends, questions, etc.

You don't have to join these boards to read the discussions and learn from others in similar circumstances. You may also discover some ways to save you never considered before. SAVVY Mom learned how to turn in old ink-jet cartridges for office supply store credit on one of these sites.

The important thing to remember is to keep your eyes and ears open. You can read about deals in the newspaper, hear new ideas on the news, and find stuff for yourself just surfing online. It's amazing what SAVVY Cat uncovers just snoozing near the computer. Remember to take notes and check out the tips. You may just find a bargain, save some money, or figure out how to get a super deal.

HOW TO FIND A CYBER COUPON OR CODE

It takes a couple of minutes to search for an online coupon or promotional code for a percentage off, or free shipping on an order. My morning stretch and scratch session takes more time than checking for a deal. Of course, there may be no coupons available. There might be a code for free shipping or a discount. Ten percent off a $50 item equals $5.

The following example shows two ways to find online codes for major national retailers. I selected Safeway for this example. SAVVY Mom sometimes orders goodies from them online, and they usually have a free-delivery or discount code available.

- Option A:
  Go to an online deal site such as www.dealhunting.com. In the center of the Dealhunting.com homepage there is a search box with a drop-down menu to look for online merchants. Select Safeway.com and press enter.
- Option B:
  Type the following into the search box of your web browser: wwww.safeway.com online coupon codes. (The search will offer a variety of websites that offer coupon codes for Safeway.com. This option gives you the widest variety of sites, but you may have to check several to find a current code.)
- Results:
  Both of these options listed the following information for Safeway.com. Option A listed the code which you can write down or copy by highlighting the code, EASY7, right clicking on your mouse and selecting copy. The second website offered a direct link.

Free Delivery **EASY7** Limit one use per customer. $50 minimum order required. Valid for the First Delivery Only

Whenever you shop online use this process to check for coupons or discounts. Some codes are specific to a particular type of product, exclude certain purchases, require a minimum purchase, or have a specific expiration date. Some sites neglect to edit out old coupons, but you quickly learn which forums offer accurate, up-to-date information. SAVVY CATS are discerning as well as thrifty.

HOW TO ADD A PROMO CODE TO AN ONLINE ORDER

Once you find a coupon code online what do you do with it? Most online stores ask for promotional codes near the end of the checkout process. Sometimes, promotional codes get added automatically to your shopping cart when you shop through a link provided by the retailer in an email or when you shop through a link from a deal site.

- Locate Where to Add Promotion Codes:
  Coupons and promotional codes usually get added at check out. Look for a box on the order summary page or on the page where you enter your payment information. Many sites locate the add-on box either at the top or bottom of the check-out/payment pages.

- Add the Code:
  Type or copy and paste the code where indicated. Often you click on a link that says, "Add" or "Update" coupon or promotional code. Once code gets uploaded, most sites update the shopping cart total and list the coupon or discount. If the code is incorrect or expired you will see a note that that particular code is invalid. Promotion codes may be case-sensitive, which means use caps or lower case letters as indicated.

- Confirm the Discount:
  Before you complete your transaction confirm the discount gets applied to your order. If the discount is for free shipping you may need to select the free shipping option rather than the standard shipping option which may include a fee. If there is a problem you can try re-entering the code, calling the store's customer service center, etc.

If you are having trouble the code may be invalid, typed incorrectly, or you may not have purchased the specified item or amount needed to receive the discount. Whether or not you choose to finalize the order is up to you.

Some retailers offer free shipping or free delivery to their store. You select the shipping option in the checkout process from a list or pull-down menu. Free shipping is usually the standard ground service. If you want your order shipped via overnight or second-day service you will pay extra for that convenience.

In my area, a few of the local retailers that offer free shipping to your local store include: Wal-Mart, Sears, Circuit City, REI, Office Depot, Ace Hardware, Loews, and more. If the local store is within reasonable driving distance, and convenient for you to drop by this option may save your $5 or more. SAVVY Mom combines an in-store pick-up with other errands to save time, gas and money.

CHEAP FILLERS FOR FREE SHIPPING & SAVINGS

Some online retailers offer free shipping for a minimum purchase. Office supply stores frequently include free shipping with a $50 purchase. Amazon.com offers free shipping on a wide variety of items they stock for a $25 purchase. When you cyber shop check if the store discounts shipping at certain price points.

If your purchase is close to the free shipping level, see if you can find an inexpensive item to bring your cart just over the ship it free threshold. For example, office supply stores have numerous items less than a dollar (pens, pencils, paperclips, etc.). Choose an inexpensive item you will use, add it to your cart and get the shipping discount. Your savings may range from a few dollars up to ten or more.

The same principle applies if you are close to a discount for a set value of your purchase. For example, office supply stores frequently advertise deals for $25 off a $125 purchase. SAVVY Mom often bundles purchases for ink, printer paper, and other supplies to qualify for a discount plus free shipping.

A number of deal sites have filler lists for Amazon.com and other national retailers. Look for inexpensive fillers in outlet, sale or clearance section of the retailers too. SAVVY Mom can usually find an inexpensive product or a rebate item to add to qualify for free shipping or to reach a coupon discount threshold.

REBATE YOUR WAY TO FREE PRODUCTS

You may have noticed cat's spines flex and twist easily. Of course, I need to bathe certain body parts to maintain my sweet feline aroma. Flexibility is the backbone of saving moola at the store too.

Every month many retail stores offer items for purchase with rebates. Walgreens, Rite Aid, and CVS are a couple of drugstores that have rebate programs. Other places to find rebate items include Office Depot, Office Max, Staples, etc. Many online stores have a Rebate Center with printable forms and information on current rebates. Look for rebate forms printed in newspaper store ads or inserts. In stores look for rebate tear pads near new products, at the customer service counter, or even forms attached to items. Rebate forms sport microscopic print so use a magnifier to ensure you can read the instructions and mailing information accurately.

During the past year, SAVVY Mom's free after rebate items included: a messenger style laptop bag; a math quiz calculator; a scientific calculator; an electronic Spanish dictionary; a telephone/fax combo; an X Box 360 game controller; an MP3 stereo speaker system; a wireless laptop mouse; a portable memory stick; a laptop travel pack with portable memory, mouse, USB hub and a retractable USB cord; $150 worth of Shell gas cards; plus full-size personal care and household products. Our family uses some freebies ourselves, gives them as gifts, or donates them to charity.

If you try refunding, carefully read the fine print on the forms; note specific requirements regarding mailing dates and proofs of purchase; and include any UPC's or other proofs requested. Make a copy of your submission or scan it onto your computer before you mail the refund to the company.

Most refunds are limited to one per household or address. Many ban the use of P.O. boxes. [This helps protect against fraud and abuse.] Also, do not purchase items for rebate if you are not comfortable paying the price if the rebate is rejected or lost.

Some online sites describe how to make money buying a computer or other high value item using multiple rebates, price matching, etc. Don't be sucked into thinking you can get a new laptop computer for free and make a couple of hundred on the deal. For the one psycho who is able to pull this off, a bunch of other folks waste a good deal of money on something they probably didn't need in the first place. If it sounds too good to be true it probably is.

If you are considering a complicated refund deal check out the forums of various savings websites and see if people are actually making these things work. I'd just as soon nap as spend three hours filling out forms, trotting around getting price-match rebates, copying receipts, etc.

Do not spend more money than you could afford to loose on any deal. Also remember that rebates do not include your local sales tax. Calculate the true cost of the item. Don't buy stuff you don't need or can't use productively.

Be wary of rebate deals from retailers you know are in financial trouble. Purchasing an item to get rebate that might disappear in a bankruptcy filing, risks the hard earned money you forked out. Forums in the rebate sites listed below are a good resource for up-to-date news about risky rebates and companies. In the past year even some rebate processors went belly-up.

Being smart is the hallmark of the SAVVY CAT. If a deal sounds too good to be true walk away. If you choose to pursue a deal be sure you will be happy with the full price you paid if the promised refund never arrives. Do not risk cash you are not willing to lose. Remember, rebates can take up to 12 weeks to mail so hurry up and wait.

A bit of friendly advice for the passionate rebate seeker, who loves to share a good deal with anyone who will listen; avoid loudly advertising certain sensitive rebate types in mixed company. You might think I refer to unmentionable feminine products, but no – I refer to deals involving condoms and other similar products. I dare not explain the reason for this delicate advice, but take my word for it. Your family and friends will thank you for your savvy discretion.

Some websites SAVVY Mom uses to find rebate offers include:

www.dealhack.com
www.fatwallet.com
www.freeafter.com
www.refundsweepers.com
www.slickdeals.net

SPEND MONEY MORE THAN ONCE

Spend money two times or more? Are you nuts? Should you be locked up? These thoughts cross my mind time and again as I hear the shouting, screaming and high fiving going on in my household when the mailman arrives with a cash rebate for some trinket purchased on sale, with a coupon, and a reward card no less.

I puzzled on this conundrum during my morning nap. Suddenly it dawned on me. Spending money twice! Brilliant!! What a gem of a deal! No wonder they are high fiving, dancing, and singing.

Here's what I figured during my quiet thinking. Getting a cash rebate for some little item means the money you spent once comes back to be spent yet again. Does the government know about this? You bet. It is all legal.

Use your rebates the following month to purchase additional rebate items. You use free money to buy stuff that gets you more free stuff and free money. What a concept. My tail is spinning at the thought of this money multiplying plan. Given the right planning you could buy freebies with free money for an entire year for a free, free, free fest at the holidays.

You go, girl! Make those dollars dance once, twice, and even thrice!! What a thrill. No wonder I love my life!

ONLINE REWARD PROGRAMS

I love rewards, whether it's an extra bit of tuna on my plate or a free gift card to the local feline emporium. There are oodles of online reward programs. These sites might give you points for reading emails advertisers send, that reward you with bonuses for shopping or searching through their website. One site rewards members with cold hard cash toward college expenses and other educational needs.

I like a couple of different sites in particular, but there are many available to choose from. My favorites are www.mypoints.com and www.upromise.com.

For example, My Points gives rewards for taking surveys, shopping, travel, reading emails, and other activities. Over the last eight years or so SAVVY Mom redeemed over 50,000 points on this website. That amounts to over $450 dollars in free gift cards, donations to charity, etc.

SAVVY Mom combines the point offers on this site with online coupons whenever possible, plus she pays for purchases or travel with a credit card that grants points toward gift cards, hotel nights, car rentals, plane tickets, etc.

The cumulative rewards from all the sources can be substantial. Use these freebies to stretch your budget, a special purchase, gifts, or a free night out.

How do they work? Retailers pay the websites for directing customers to their online stores. You access the retailer through a link on the reward site. The reward site may ask you to register your credit or debit card in order to track your purchases. When you shop through their link and make a purchase, the reward site gives you a portion of the commission they get from the retailer. The size of your reward gets based on the value of your purchase. Your bonus might be points per dollars spent or some other premium. Depending on the site you choose your reward may be gift cards, merchandise, or cash back.

Not all reward sites are created equal. You need to look at how you will use the site. If you shop online, check to see if your favorite retailer participates with a particular program. SAVVY Mom uses different reward programs based on where she shops online.

In many cases, you can stack these rewards with the retailer's online coupons or promotional offers. For example, a retailer sends a promotional code for free shipping, or some other discount in an email or catalog. Write down the promotional code, check if that retailer participates with one of the reward programs you use.

For example, if I am going to shop at store XYZ I start at www.mypoints.com, log-on, and check if that store is one of their merchant affiliates. If it is I click on the link from mypoints.com to the store and do my shopping. If I have a promotional code I add it during the checkout process. Once I complete my purchase, the amount gets recorded and my My Points account receives credit a few days or weeks later. Once I have enough points I convert them to the gift card of my choice. Most reward/rebate sites operate in a similar manner.

It sounds a complicated at first, but once you catch on to the routine you will find it pretty straightforward. I view these as bonuses for savvy surfing. When shopping online use a credit card that offers its own rewards to pay for your purchases. SAVVY Mom likes to stack as many rewards as possible.

You may just get points from the shopping affiliate site, possibly coupon discount, and then a points or cash-back for each dollar spent using the credit card. Once you get used to thinking this way you will look ways to save as much as possible. Save up rewards and redeem them for free gifts at the holidays, gas, a dinner out, hotels, airline flights, etc.

SAVVY Mom prefers to use a couple of sites more often, but there are others that might suit you better. Remember, you are more likely to use a reward site regularly if it meets your needs and offers incentives you will use. If you find a great site share it with your friends and family. Here are a few we've used over the years.

www.erewards.com
www.fatwallet.com
www.mypoints.com
www.upromise.com

YOU PROMISE WHAT? FREE MONEY FOR EDUCATION?

Free is free, as far as I'm concerned. How about free money for college? If you are out of college how about free money to help pay down those loads of loans?

No loans, no kids in college how about free money to help your favorite grandson or nephew with his college expenses? Even the childless, friendless curmudgeon down the street can get free money for his favorite educational institution. Just think of it as free money to keep those nasty rug rats in school, off the streets, and out of your hair.

My cross-species brother accumulated enough free money to purchase his expensive math books for one quarter. That amounted to almost $400. All those little bits and pieces 1% here 3% there add up over time. UPromise offers national, regional and local deals. The program adds new retailers and services all the time.

You can search by zip code for restaurants, groceries, drugstores, and services that offer deals in your area. Your reward might be anywhere from a set amount to a percentage of your total expenditures. Restaurants offer rewards of anywhere from four to eight percent of your total bill. Make your vacation or business travel arrangements through the companies linked to their site and get one or two percent back on your trip.

If you shop at places like Albertsons, Fred Meyer, Safeway, or QFC (check your local stores), you register your club/discount card and your savings for purchases of sponsor's products are automatically calculated each time you shop and added to your account—AMAZING!!!

In some areas UPromise even offers auto, insurance and real-estate rewards and services. A growing number of financial institutions are linking their 529 College Savings Plans to the program allowing easy transfer of accumulated funds from your UPromise account.

Who wouldn't love a deal like that? Run to your computer and sign up at www.upromise.com today. It's easy. Too much trouble you say? I say if you think it's too much trouble to spend an extra minute or so clicking through a link to get some free money then you are either foolish or love to spend money. In my family we spend money, but like to get added value for what we spend.

Register your credit card or debit card or sign up for an UPromise credit card and save even more. Only you know your comfort level, but there are numerous options from which to choose. You may already use many of the products or services listed. Of course this is just the tip of the iceberg; the number of companies and products affiliated with this program grows all the time.

The site also has a way to ask friends and relatives to sign up and save for your favorite student or school. Just think how all those bits and pieces could compound for free money for educational expenses or your favorite school.

This is free money. If you use a credit card with its own rewards program you get your UPromise cash and still get your card's rewards points too. That's double dipping at its finest. If you are lucky you can combine a promotional coupon code or a grocery coupon for added savings. What a deal!

Now that my boy is in college our family uses UPromise to save money for our toddler cousin. Just think, what a nice high school graduation gift that will be, especially since it's free. So far we've accumulated close to $50 for the little tot. I can hardly imagine the high fiving, glad handing, and cheering when he graduates from high school about 16 years from now.

PLAY THE SAVINGS BALLGAME

Everyone yammers about the benefits of exercise. How about combining the thrill of a game, mental exercise, and thrifty spending? Get the whole family involved. Play the Savings Ballgame.

Anyhow, the game is easy to learn. The teams in my home league hold records for grand slams and home runs. Here's a run-down of the rules.

Step up to the plate and to get a single, purchase an item on sale. This gets you to first base. Of course any major leaguer knows you won't win a game on a single. Purchase a sale item with a coupon and you've managed a double. Or as an alternative, purchase a sale item with a credit card that rewards purchases with points that you can later redeem for cash, gift cards, or services.

A triple is one form of double plus an additional discount; free shipping, a rebate, or an online discount code. A home run is any combination of discounts plus some other goody. A Grand Slam happens about as frequently as it does in a real baseball game, but it entails a sale item, discounts, rewards, and a rebate. The end result is you got the item free, you got rewards, and you made cash on the deal at the end. High fives everyone! The great thing about this game is that no matter what you do you are a winner.

Just this morning Mummy stocked up on toilet paper, laundry detergent, shampoo, band aids, chips and other items. She combined a 10% Target pharmacy discount, $35 in paper coupons, plus two $5 Target Gift card freebies she got for purchasing huge amounts of my cross-species brother's favorite shampoo. Plus she purchased (with coupons of course) $14.49 worth of healthcare items to send for reimbursement to her FSA account for health spending. Overall, a savings of almost 50% on household items we use everyday. She also scored a free 16 ounce bag of the latest kitty kibble treats and some free candy. Life is gooooood in my hoooood today!

That shouting and chest thumping I mentioned at the beginning of my book is best practiced at the Savings Ballgame Stadium. Where is that located you ask? I think in my living room, but I suppose, for a nominal fee, I could allow you to franchise your own stadium. Send me a letter of interest and a blank check. I'll set you up today!

HOW MUCH CAN SAVVY CATS REALLY SAVE?

The savings you expect at the checkout counter can vary. SAVVY CAT Mom can usually shave 20% to 30% off grocery visits with minimal effort using a combination of sales only and/or sales plus a few coupons. With an investment of about an hour or so of planning time those savings can hit up to 40% or a bit more.

Even if you don't want to invest time, scanning the store ad and planning menus around items on sale will cut your overall bill. Remember $10 saved at the grocery store each week adds up to $520 in reduced spending at the end of the year.

Getting the most for your buck is what SAVVY folks do. Some examples from SAVVY Cat's recent shopping exploits include:

Deal 1: One first Tuesday of the month SAVVY Mom went to Rite Aid to pick up the monthly rebate items plus some other things we needed. After the First Tuesday discount (about 20%), coupons, and rebates, she shaved 48% or $51.16 off the total bill.

On this trip she picked up name and store brand products including: a bottle of wine, a 5 pack of premium water filters, a large jar of cashews, beef jerky, deodorant, two packs of freezer bags, 2 boxes of over-the-counter medicine, body wash, hair styling spray, candy etc.

Deal 2: SAVVY Dad wanted a 20" TV for his new, basement *Man Land.* SAVVY Mom searched online deals for tube televisions since those cost less. She checked retailers such as Circuit City, Best Buy, Kmart, Sears, Target and so on. After finding some possible choices at those websites she used an online comparison shopping tool to look for other stores that might offer similar models. Low and behold Office Depot sells a leading name-brand tube TV at one of the lowest prices. Who would have thought to look at an office supply store for a cheap TV?

Undaunted by the unusual location SAVVY Mom popped open her favorite search engine and typed in "Office Depot online coupon promo codes." About eight possibilities popped up. It took about five minutes and several tries to find a code that covered a technology purchase. In the end SAVVY Mom got free shipping on the TV, plus two gift certificates for large Papa John's pizza pies. She also paid with a credit card that will net her more goodies on down the line. Pizza party in Man Land next Friday night!!

Deal 3: SAVVY Mom did her daily check on one of her favorite deal sites, www.slickdeals.net, and spied a hot, hot deal. Sears and the Dockers brand offered a $75 Shell gas card as a rebate for purchasing $100 worth of Dockers men's apparel and accessories. The clothes were deeply discounted too. She ordered loads of cheap T-shirts and boxers for the guys, paid with one of her reward credit cards, and sent in the rebate. The other day, the gas card arrived along with a bonus store coupon for $10 off a $50 Sears' menswear purchase.

As you can see flexibility, research, and creativity can add up to some decent deals. Stay alert and take a few minutes to check out local sale flyers, online sales, rebates, and coupons. With the economy tanking, more retailers offer deep discounts, rebates, or promotions to attract buyers. This will continue through the upcoming year.

Just remember, a deal is only a deal if you can afford it, you do not pay for it with credit (unless you pay the card off religiously each month), you do not need the money for essential living expenses and it is something you need or will use. Mindless spending to get anything just because it's cheap defeats the purpose of being a SAVVY CAT.

In addition to these tangible savings add the savings you accumulate by reducing everyday expenses whether it involves switching to generic prescriptions, eating out less, visiting the library, or riding public transportation. If you need inspiration add up some of these cut-backs/savings and bask in the glory of being one SAVVY CAT!

SAVVY MOM'S JANUARY – FEBRUARY 2009 SAVINGS SUMMARY*

Rebates Received	$_66
Paper & Online Coupons	$430
Free Gift Cards Received	$105
TOTAL:	$601

*This total does not include free shipping discounts, club card sales prices, or pending rebates submitted.

As you can see from the chart above, the savings add up. Even if your results are much more modest, you can see the savings add up over time. Some months are better than others, but over the course of the year even small efforts can pay off if you add it up.

TREAT YOURSELF OCCASSIONALLY

Ok, I know avoiding restaurant or fast-food dining seems as impossible as me avoiding fishy foods. If you want to treat yourself do it the right way. Take advantage of coupons and specials.

THE SAVVY CAT'S GUIDE

Join the early bird crowd. As far as I know they don't serve worms to those early birds. They offer up dining specials to fill the restaurants during off-peak times. Some people don't want to eat that early, but consider it a late lunch and then have a light meal for dinner.

The over 21-set can seek out happy hour deals in their local watering hole. Half-price drinks and appetizers can equal a cheap, festive meal if you are old enough to partake legally. Just remember to designate a sober driver before you hit the bar.

Take advantage of coupons and other reduced cost dining deals. Every fall the Entertainment books go on sale at various charities, schools, and retail outlets. The cost of the book varies ($25-$35) in most locales. Be sure to check that you will use the coupons it contains. Better, yet, if you can defer your purchase until the summer the books drop drastically in price in June or July. I picked an extra book up for $5 this summer. Also, check out www.entertainment.com to preview your local book, and find additional printable online savings.

Another great site to check is www.restaurant.com where you can purchase discounted gift certificates to participating restaurants in your hood. This site frequently offers additional promotional discounts so search for promo codes or online coupons prior to your purchase. Just be certain to follow the ordering restrictions or requirements for the specific locale. Use your rewards credit card to pay for your meal and get additional value for your expenditure.

The aforementioned www.upromise.com also has a way to save money for college while dining out. You can find participating restaurants by searching by zip code on that site. Just remember to register the credit or debit card you use to pay for your meals out. The savings range from 4% to 8% of your total bill. Yum Yum!

Before you dine, check the website for the restaurant you plan to visit. You may find that they have a frequent diner program or offer an online coupon for a free appetizer, entrée, or desert. At the very least you can preview the menu, find a map to their exact location and a phone number to call for reservations.

Also check out your local zoo, science center or children's museum to see if their annual family plans offer a bargain of year-long entertainment. These annual family passes can pay for themselves after two or three visits. If you have one of these in your town or nearby, this could be a great source of family education and fun time after time throughout the year.

Remember it is also a great gift to give to young families. THE SAVVY CAT gave his toddler cousin a household pass to the local zoological society leading to a year of multiple visits and free companion/guest visits for a year. What a deal!!!! Not only was puss generous he managed to keep that sticky-fingered toddler occupied for long periods so he could nap uninterrupted. What a deal!!!

www.entertainment.com
www.restaurant.com
www.upromise.com/dining

FIND THE LOWEST PRICE FOR GAS IN YOUR TOWN

With a little work find the lowest price for gas in your town. Several websites track local gas prices, some offer email alerts or cell-phone alerts. These sites gather price information, identify specific stations, and frequently offer maps and driving directions.

Two sites SAVVY Mom found easy to navigate were: www.gasprices.mapquest.com and www.gasbuddy.com. Mapquest.com has a gas icon at the top of the web page. Click on that and it will open another page that asks for your location to find gas prices in your area.

Gasbuddy.com offers information for the U.S. and Canada. Just remember the prices are updated on a regular basis, but not necessarily each day. Some sites rely on reports from members. Of course if a gas station typically has the lowest price in the area, chances are you will not be disappointed even if the price is slightly higher or lower than what you saw online.

When you travel, more and more hotels offer use of a computer in their lobby or some sort of internet access. The great thing is that you can use those to check local gas deals too.

www.gasbuddy.com
www.gasprices.mapquest.com

OFFICE AND SCHOOL SUPPLY DEALS

Bargains abound in the office and school supply arena. All the major retailers (Office Max, Office Depot, Staples, etc.) offer promotional coupons, loss-leader sale items, rebates both in-store and online.

Every summer these stores cut the price of school necessities to unreal levels. Recently SAVVY Mom got penny and nickel rulers, protractors, folders, erasers, and other goodies. These are going to the local charity for their annual school supply distribution to low-income families.

One day she scored $31 retail worth of goodies for $0.82. Here's what she did. The local Office Depot offers a $3 store credit for each ink jet cartridge recycled through their store. Only specific types qualify so call your local retailer and see if your brand is included in the deal.

At my local Office Depot they allow customers to turn in up to 25 cartridges per day. The clerk printed out one $3 store credit slip per cartridge. You can use three coupons, or $9 worth of the credit per day, on a purchase total of $9.01 pre-sales tax or more. Combine those credit slips with sales, rebates, or other deals to maximize your savings.

Office supply stores also carry various supplies such as coffee, paper towels, TP and cleaning supplies. If those items are on sale their price may be comparable to what you pay elsewhere. Anyway, if you choose your purchases carefully you can walk out for a dollar or two with bags loaded with free or near free goodies.

The last trip we made included more school supplies, garage sale supplies, envelopes, and a scientific calculator with a rebate. On that trip $30 worth of items will cost less than $5, after the ink cartridge credits and the rebate. Again, the bulk of the items will go to help kiddies go to school with new supplies.

These same office supply retailers routinely offer online discount coupons and free shipping for all orders over $50. Sometimes the promotions are as high as $20 off a $75 order. There are usually restrictions on what may be purchased with the coupon discount, but we stock up on ink cartridges and other expensive items when they are included in the discount. Again, use your rewards credit card to seal the deal and get bonus points as well.

While online sign up to receive emails and snail mail promotions. These stores regularly send out coupons for in-store and online purchases. Office Max sometimes offers $10 off a $20 in-store purchase. Again, combine these discounts with sales or other promotions and get the most for your money. If you do not need the coupon, pass it on to someone who can use it, you may even want to ask your child's teacher or school if they want it.

SAMPLE YOUR WAY THROUGH TSA

Do you travel? Do you spend $1 or more for travel-size toiletries of 3 ounces or less that fit into the regulation one quart Ziploc bags required to pass through security at the airport? Stop wasting time, money and effort looking for those small containers. Get the goodies for free.

Manufacturer's often offer samples of their products for us to try free. You can find links to free samples on manufacturer's web sites, or attached to full-size products you find at the store. Save those little goodies and use them on your next trip.

Over the course of several months Mummy collected mini toothpaste, make-up, deodorant, and shampoo samples and stored them in the linen closet in a little box. She even got a free toothbrush from the hotel clerk for the asking when she went out of town overnight. You can also stockpile samples to bridge the gap for a few days if you run out of shampoo, toothpaste, detergent or other items.

The up side of all of this is that she had all the little goodies she needed to last for several trips. The beauty of this situation multiplied when she whizzed through the security line with her little Ziploc baggy filled with useful and security approved freebies.

The biggest bonus, you dump as you go. Finish one little tube of toothpaste and dump it in the garbage. Your little zipper bag gets lighter as you go and you don't have to lug sloppy containers around in your suitcase. You can also leave the remnants of these little gems when you return home and not waste cash. You got the goodies free after-all.

SAVING TO HELP OTHERS

I must admit altruism does not come naturally to cats. Humans, however, often empathize with people and animals less fortunate than themselves. Studies show that proportionally lower income families give the most to charitable causes.

Some people tell me they don't have space to store 10 free bottles of shampoo or loads of nearly free school supplies. I say, OK, no problem. You can still get the deal and then pass it on to some cat that can use it. You can be generous, but no one need know you spent nothing or just pennies on the dollar.

You can also give great gifts to folks without spending a fortune. I gave my cross-species niece an expensive Cross Pen as a college graduation gift. No need to volunteer I got 75% off before I plunked down the cash.

The stockpile of freebies and rebate items can be used to help others. Shelters can use sample-size shampoos and lotions. Plastic storage bags help homeless folks keep clothing and personal belongings dry in rainy weather. That extra free ketchup or soup can help a local food bank keep shelves stocked. The free samples of cat food, dog food (perish the thought) can help the local animal shelter. The sale rulers, protractors, and notebooks can help kids who don't have much go to school with new supplies. The possibilities are endless.

If a birthday, graduation or anniversary celebrations lay, in your future, ask for donations of food for a food bank, goodies for an animal shelter, etc. Most of us have too much stuff already, plus the whole point of having a party is to get together, have fun, and enjoy each other's company. You can even set a $3 limit on the item. The person who gets the most for their money could win a special prize or award. Go have some fun and help others at the same time.

All these things can be done inexpensively or for free. On this note think what you can do not just for yourself, but others as well. Just think if all of us picked up a couple of freebies and pass them on to those in need the world will be a better place.

CRAIGSLIST, 2 GOOD 2 TOSS, &FREECYLCE

Talk about bargains. These three websites top my list if I am looking for goodies cheap. Just about everyone's heard of the Craigslist phenomenon. You can find housing, work, and loads of stuff. Some of it is free for the asking. We unloaded a few excess goodies here for cash, and found out about some great opportunities to save money and make money too.

SAVVY Mom checks out part-time jobs, services wanted and gigs. She got $50 recently for a 90 minute consumer focus group at a local hotel. She parked free, got free pop and got an envelope with cash at the end. SAVVY Mom also got to share her views on local utility rates and billing plans too. She's opinionated and loves to talk, a win win situation for both parties.

Every other year or so, we have a garage sale in order to unload junk we no longer use. Do not spend $20 for a basic garage sale ad in the local paper. List your garage sale on Craigslist. It's free to sign up, you write your own ad, and you can even upload pictures. The step by step instructions are easy to follow. So many people use Craigslist in my area that we get good traffic to our sales.

Write a clever ad title and people will read your posting. One year it was "Desperate Housewives Sell Hubby's Stuff." This year it was, *Three Gals and their Junk, 2 Pack-Rats Trying to Reform + 1 Who Loves a Great Sale – Come Find out Who is Who.*

Another great place to hunt for goods or inexpensive services in my area is 2 Good 2 Toss. This service focuses on keeping used, but still useable goods out of our local landfills. The concept is great. You post deals on items you would otherwise take to the dump. There is usually a limit on what you can charge for an item. In our house we saved a treadmill, mattresses, and computer items from being dumped. The site tabulates the volume of trash diverted from the dump. It is a win, win situation. This site limits the price of items for sale to less than $99.

The Freecycle Network is another great resource for gently used items. Check online to find if any groups participate in this barter/exchange program in your town. Freecycle events do not allow cash exchanges, just free swaps or give-a-ways.

You might even consider starting a free exchange with friends in your neighborhood, workplace, church, or school. SAVVY Mom even heard of an exchange set up in a dorm where students exchanged gently used clothes, shoes, accessories and jewelry for a coupon to buy "new" stuff from other students in the same dorm. What a great idea!!!

These sites can save a few bucks, help mother earth, help people less fortunate, and reuse lots of goodies until they truly wear out. Most require you register for an account. Of course that too is free. You can use your "savvy email" for this type of deal too. If you advertise an item on the web select the anonymous reply option so you don't have to give out personal information to anyone who happens to read your posting.

Just remember to practice safe surfing. Scammers abound in cyberspace. If someone offers to purchase an item to send to their friend in some third world country, and promises you big bucks to cover shipping and handling, don't fall for the bait. If you are purchasing a big item and carrying a large amount of cash be smart and meet the seller or buyer in the parking lot of the local police substation or some other busy public place.

Once when I tried to sell a trendy pocket bike I got offers that said "I'll trade for your item with some good stuff on the down low." Being the Savvy Cat I recognized this was not an offer of free catnip, but something less desirable and very likely illegal. Needless to say I thanked that dude for his interest, but replied I just wanted cash not "down low" goodies.

The beauty of all this is that you can practice your street talk, recycle your junk, and sometimes make a bit of cash. What a deal! That's being one SAVVY CAT!

CLOTHING DEALS

Any parent will tell you that kids grow faster than their clothes wear out. The whole family can cut costs by shopping for clothing at local thrift stores, garage sales, and consignment shops or perhaps participating in some type of free exchange.

Goodwill, Bargain World, St. Vincent de Paul, and Value Village advertise weekly and sometimes daily deals on a large variety of used clothing. Many items are so gently used they look new. All of these stores have 99 cent deals or half-price sales regularly. See what's available in your area and scope it out. Almost new, name-brand clothing abounds if you dig through the racks.

Also remember to clean out your closets and make a donation. Many of these stores will give you a tax deductible receipt, or a discount coupon for shopping at their store. Just don't give the stores torn, dirty junk. If you wouldn't be caught dead in that ratty t-shirt, no one else wants it either. Plus, your so-called charitable donation will end up in the landfill and the thrift store gets nailed for the fee.

Consignment stores tend to have slightly higher prices, but usually their items look nearly new and many carry higher end name brands. If you have clean, quality clothes to sell you might check these out and make a few bucks selling clothes you no longer wear, or clothes your kids have outgrown. Of course these stores have markdowns and sales too. One children's consignment store in my town offers huge 25 cent bargain tables the last Friday and Saturday of the month. The frenzy at their store on those days reminds me of water frothing schools of piranha eating some hapless victim.

Another SAVVY option is to follow department store and outlet sales. Many have regular clearance events and some offer additional discounts off the lowest clearance price. SAVVY Friend shops for designer duds at Ross and other discount retailers. She finds cheap deals at Ross and then takes hubby to shop, but only on Tuesdays. That's the day her youthful looking, senior husband (60+) gets an additional 10% off any purchase. The store doesn't care who slips them the cash. They just want the clothes out the door. SAVVY Dad is counting the days until he gets his AARP badge to wear.

Take the time to educate yourself about your town. Look in the yellow pages for consignment, thrift, or resale stores. Look on the internet and ask your SAVVY friends. The cost of one new department store outfit can translate into a wardrobe of gently used, nearly new name-brand duds.

USPS SNAIL MAIL SECRETS

If you are in the know, you know what I know; that USPS stands for the United States Postal Service or snail mail in techno speak. SAVVY Mom works the mail system to save cold hard cash. She learned these techniques by unloading some things on EBay and learning how to mail packages for the lowest cost worldwide.

We can easily say no to the outrageous cost of overnight mail, but those clever governmental postal kingpins dangle a prize even more precious, Priority Mail Service. Americans hate to wait so many choose this economical 2-3 day service. It's a great service for many items, but did you know that you might save a $1 or more off the Priority Mail price when sending packages weighing 13 oz. or less by shipping via the First Class Parcel rate?

Also, have you ever noticed the bright, colorful specialty envelopes and rainbow hued packing materials located strategically within arms reach of the slow paced, snail mail queue? Perhaps you picked up a $3 flower covered padded mailer for Auntie Em's birthday gift, and added a matching address label for another half-dollar or so? How sweet! If you select Priority Mail service, kick yourself for wasting about 4 bucks?

DON'T BE DAZZLED BY THIS DANGEROUS CONSUMER BAIT!!! The SAVVY Snail Mailer knows the real prize lies just beyond this masterful marketing display. Imagine how tickled Auntie would be with a more expensive birthday gift mailed to her in a free, yes, free Priority Mail envelope or box, addressed with the free, yes, free

Priority Mail label? She'd think you were the best niece or nephew on the planet and would likely increase your payout in her will just because you know the value of a buck.

Why place those pretty packages first? Why employ only two or three counter clerks even at the busiest of times? Why ask a litany of questions about the contents of your packages and if you need stamps? The whole plot is designed to slow you down, numb your senses to get you to buy, buy, and buy some more!

So walk past those sweet displays, pick up a load of free mailing supplies, and walk out the door knowing you are one savvy consumer. If you pay taxes you've already paid for those boxes so use them with impunity. As a bonus, you can pretend you're pulling off a fast one on the government.

A Word of Caution: Use the free packaging materials as intended. Do not swipe the free Priority Mail boxes and try to cover the logos or use the boxes for Media Mail or Parcel Post. SAVVY Mom witnessed the apparent glee with which the usually down-trodden postal clerks pounce upon such violations. You can kiss your pre-paid postage goodbye if you printed your own label from home too. That's Postal Payback for all the snarky comments and complaints these dedicated government employees endure daily. If you try to cheat the USPS you deserve a sharp, pointed swat in my humble opinion.

Before I leave postal paradise, check out those fabulous multi-sized flat-rate Priority Mail boxes. These too are free, but you can load those suckers with as much weight as they can hold up to the maximum and still close neatly. I once sent dear Auntie Em a new set of free weights in a standard size flat rate box for a fee of $9.80. Those 20 lb. babies would have cost me a fortune to mail in a regular Priority Mail box, but they fit purrfectly in one of the 4 sizes of flat-rate boxes. I saved a bundle and ensured Auntie can work out and continue to lift cases of tuna into her car from her grocery cart.

The US government offers its biggest flat-rate box at a discount if you when shipping to APO & FPO addresses. SUPPORT OUR TROOPS with a care package at a bargain rate. The beauty of those flat rate envelopes and boxes is that you can send them to other countries too. Just pay the international rate, but the flat rate generally beats the price of other mailing options. Confirm size, content and weight restrictions for individual countries. Also, fill out your customs forms before you get to the counter.

If you don't want to bother lugging those priority boxes, labels, and other mailing forms home go online to www.usps.com, order your supplies at the Postal

Store and get them delivered to your home for free. This website offers all you need to be your own purrsonal postal guru.

Did you buy a gross of those Forever Stamps before 5/12/08? I sure did, or at least my people did. Let's just say they stashed a load of those precious 41 cent mailing gems in a great hiding place. The place is so good, I can't remember it at the moment, but that worries me none. As a matter of fact that is all part of the plan. By the time they unearth those little gems they'll be worth a fortune. I just hope I live to see that glorious day. The next big rate hike is scheduled for May 2009. If you missed out on this deal the first time, stock up at 42 cents a pop and beat the price increase.

www.usps.com

MOVING?

When most people hear that phrase they think boxes, packing, U-Haul trucks, etc. At my age, "moving" means I'm still alive. My purrsonal vet no longer refers to me as a senior puss, now she calls me geriatric. I called AARP to start a protest petition, but they blatantly discriminate against cats if you can believe that in this day and age. Of course you didn't buy this book to find out if I was still breathing, so enough about me.

The expense of moving, coupled with the cost of settling into a new household means coupons and specials abound. If you are renting a truck, or using a moving company, ask if there are off-peak days or times. You might be able to schedule your departure to take advantage of mid-week, mid-month specials in your area. Remember, weekends and the beginning and end of the month are busiest so truck rentals generally cost more.

Do not buy boxes if you can avoid the expense. One night while patrolling my hood in my custom Catmobile, a very fuel efficient vehicle I might add, I noticed the local UPS store had an open recycling bin with loads of boxes awaiting a new life. These flat boxes were not crushed, just flat. Keep your eyes peeled in your local commercial district and near your home, you may get lucky, especially the night before recycling pick-up.

If you would rather not take boxes from private recycling bins then visit your local liquor store or ask all your friends and neighbors. Focus on prospects, like my family, who wave at the local delivery driver when they see them on the street. In other words, look for those types who spend copious amounts of time online scouting for deals. They have boxes coming out of their ears and would likely be happy to unload them on you.

As for other deals, start at the local Post Office, the government has a snazzy moving kit crammed full of mailing forms and, somewhat surprisingly, discounts from places like Loews, Home Depot, Best Buy, etc. Of course Big Brother uses these pretty folders and discounts to keep tabs on where you are moving, but I suppose you would still like to receive your subscriptions to Cat Cuisine and Cats Outside each month so, it's a fair trade-off.

When my cross-species brother recently abandoned ship and moved into his own luxury studio apartment he discovered he could command 10% off at some of those retailers just because he changed his zip code. Of course, they hope you buy the biggest flat screen TV they stock, but it might come in handy for smaller items too, for example, power cords, wireless hubs, etc.

Also investigate deals on apartments and rentals online. Many websites such as www.apartments.com and www.rent.com let you search listings by state, region, town, area, or zip code. Some offer rewards if you sign a lease with one of their clients. The amount varies, but it might be $100 or more. Craigslist is another great resource. It offers extensive listings for rentals, shared housing, etc.

Don't forget to ask landlords if they have any deals or specials to entice you to sign a lease. Many list that information on their websites. The bro got 2 free months rent and 6 months free parking with his 12 month lease. It made his fancy digs seem like a bargain.

As with everything else, keep your eyes and ears open. Ask anyone who will listen if they can help ease the stress and expense of your move. You may unearth some out-of-this world advice that will save you loads. Just be discerning, that big, tattooed guy on the barstool next to you might not be offering you a deal if he volunteers to send you to the moon for free. Happy packing!

HOW TO GET THE LOWEST PRICE ON A CAR

SAVVY Mom found the last four vehicles our family purchased. She checked out the deals, and negotiated to her target price. Just like stores, dealers often advertise a loss leader vehicle to get you on their lot. There is usually only one available and the early bird gets the worm.

SAVVY Dad scored a cheap Toyota pick-up on one of these deals. He plopped my then 2 year old cross-species brother in the bed of the lone $6,000 truck to claim his stake. Fortunately no one drove off with bro in the back of the truck. The salesman couldn't believe the price was so low, but he checked with the Manager and it was.

The next car purchase was over the phone. Again, it was a loss-leader deal. Mummy bought the new car sight unseen. The dealer tried to get her to consider other models, but she was insistent. She even told the dealer, "Do you want to sell a car or not? I'm telling you I will buy it over the phone. You don't have to do any work. I can't believe you don't want such an easy deal." Anyway, they ultimately came to an understanding. Again, the deal was within the target price found doing research. The next purchase was made online, just when internet car sales were starting to take off. The local Subaru dealer offered a special discount for cars sold via internet contact.

In the days before the internet, car deals were advertised on television and in the newspaper. A good time to purchase a vehicle is in the summer when dealers need to clear stock to make room for the new model year vehicles. Cash talks at the end of the month or end of the fiscal year too. If you find an unreal deal it is probably limited to one car, identified by its VIN number. The early bird scores the deal.

Today, research is the best way to get a deal on a car. Consumer Reports is a great place to start researching car prices, reliability, miles per gallon, insurance costs and so on. Once you have identified the make, year and model of the vehicle you want use dealer websites, and price comparison sites to identify the target price for your negotiations. Use the many resources available to research your car before you step on the dealer's lot and you will be able to make an intelligent assessment of the purchase rather than an emotional one. Cars lose a significant portion of their value the minute you drive off the lot. A low-mileage, certified, used car can save thousands of dollars. Just be sure to ask the dealer for a vehicle history report.

Our most recent purchase was a vehicle for my cross-species bro. Three months of research paid off. The dealer was stunned when SAVVY Mom questioned why the sticker price was $3500 more than the online price. The salesman told her, "Don't worry about the price on the sticker, that's just markup." Needless to say we got the Cruiser just slightly above our bottom-line target price.

The beauty of doing the research ahead of time means that you can tell if a sale or offer is truly a deal the minute you get on the lot. Salesmen hope you will be dazzled by gaudy goo gaws and bells and whistles. Get over the pretty doo dads and bargain your way to a decent deal. You do not necessarily have to pay for extras the dealer added to your vehicle before they put it on the lot. Most items are negotiable, especially now they need to move cars. Dealers love to tell you they will go broke offering deals like you want, but hang tough. Walk if you must, but you'll probably get a deal.

Also, secure your own financing for the purchase. If you do have sterling credit you will get the lowest rate regardless of where you get the loan. Don't be sucked into the dealer asking you what kind of payment you would like. Any loan deal can be tweaked in terms of the length to get the numbers you want. When SAVVY Mom's friends got a car, the dealer nearly had a conniption when she slyly asked what interest rate and loan term the monthly payment represented. The dealer replied it was 9% for 72 months. Needless to say, they had already secured a quote of 6% over 48 months from their credit union. Guess which loan they selected?

Websites like www.carfax.com allow you to search for a detailed history of used vehicles by the VIN number. This report will detail the history of that specific vehicle including the number of owners, accidents, repairs, etc. The car dealer should provide you with this report free of charge, but if they don't volunteer the information, ask. You can find it yourself, but if the dealer is less than forthcoming take that as a sign to move on.

New cyber deals for cars include folks advertising to get out of their lease. This is similar to folks trying to get out from under cell contracts. This relatively new service, www.leasetrader.com allows folks to advertise (for a fee) and ~~unload~~ transfer a car lease they no longer want. This service popped up in response to folks looking for affordable lease deals and others wanting to ~~dump~~ sign over vehicles they no longer want. If you decide you just have to have that fancy leased goodie, make sure the mileage restrictions, cost, and term fit your needs.

www.carfax.com
www.cars.com
www.edmunds.com
www.leasetrader.com
www.motoralley.com

FIND THE CHEAPEST CAR TO INSURE

When the cross-species bro turned 15 we contacted our insurance agent, and asked how adding a young male driver would impact our rates. SAVVY Dad choked when he heard the response. Smelling salts quickly revived SAVVY Dad, but we had work to do.

First, we searched the internet for local driving instruction schools and found a place that had summer classes and cost $199 vs. $450 for the name-brand course heavily advertised at the time. Second, we searched the internet for months trying to find an economical car, with adequate room for him and all his guitars, amps, and musical equipment.

Several vehicles fit the bill, but which one cost the least over the life of the car? SAVVY Mom finally found a site that helped sort through the hype. Getting a deal on the price of the car may feel good, but finding a car that will cost you less to repair, operate and insure for life thrills me to the core. Ultimately we purchased a PT Cruiser, one of the cheapest to insure. Our rates tripled, but the choice of car combined with our teen getting his license at 18 rather than 16, saved thousands.

When your new car's warranty runs out, AAA is a great deal for emergency roadside assistance. The annual membership costs less than a tow and you are covered for just about any breakdown, or keys locked in the car inconvenience. AAA also offers bonus savings. They negotiate low rates at hotels and motels nationwide, exchange cash for foreign currency at some of the best rates around, and arrange for member discounts on entertainment and shopping too.

www.carinsurance.com
www.aaa.com

BARGAIN WAREHOUSE FEVER

Membership warehouse clubs (Costco or Sam's Club) may or may not be a deal for you. All clubs offer unbelievable deals on some items. If their deals are the best price you can get on something you need or use, great. They offer members discounts on cars, insurance, and other major purchases. Costco even sells caskets for the thrifty funeral supply shopper.

Just remain vigilant. Those big cavernous stores with the heavy flat trolleys instead of carts project an image that bigger is better and volume means low-cost. You can get snookered into spending too much on something that sells cheaper at your local retailer.

The president of my kitty fan club got taken in by a twin-pack of trendy, antioxidant laden pomegranate juice. The warehouse club price was $17 a bottle. Of course, SAVVY Cat pointed out that the local gourmet grocery up the block had a similar item for $5.99. One would assume the specialty grocery would be higher in price than Costco, but not always.

My family tried a membership for a year and found it did not meet our needs. Your situation may be different. Just keep your eyes open and don't assume everything is a bargain.

Friends or neighbors with membership club cards may invite you along occasionally when they go shopping, but don't ask to tag along uninvited. If you want to shop the club, go to customer service and get a one-day pass. You will pay about 5-10% more than club members, but at least you pay your own way versus piggy-backing on a member.

In most locations Costco, will allow non-members to use their pharmacy and optometric services. Just call to compare their price for prescriptions, etc. You may save a few bucks even if you do not spring for an annual membership.

> Dr. C's WAREHOUSE CLUB SAFETY TIP:
> Keep your eyes pealed in those big stores, years ago a heavy pallet fell off a top shelf and crushed a bargain seeker. It may or may not be an urban legend, but forewarned is forearmed.

TRAVEL DEALS

Travel deals abound in cyberspace. It takes a bit of practice to find the best offers, but perseverance and research can pay handsomely in the end.

Membership rewards programs abound in the travel industry. SAVVY Mom and Dad join these free rewards programs at hotels, motels, rental car agencies, airlines and the like. You can maximize points and rewards by sticking with one or two programs and their affiliates, but the least expensive deals require a bit of flexibility.

If you are looking for airline tickets, check which major airlines fly to and from your destination. The following .com sites are useful to begin a search: Priceline, Sidestep, Orbitz, Travelocity, and Mobissimo are all easy to access and use. If you own an Entertainment book check out their travel offers. SAVVY Mom helped two friends get a discount on their American Airlines tickets using their Entertainment coupon.

This general search may show an airfare you feel is cheap, but double check with the specific airline. Some of these clearinghouse style sites charge a small fee for booking through their site. Go directly to the airline and check their price. If you have frequent flyer points see if you can use those too. Some airlines offer decent combined cash and miles fares. If you are close to the threshold for a free travel award see if you can buy miles for a reasonable charge. Also, some airlines with high volume routes will offer deals booking two one-way tickets. Try different options to uncover the best prices. SAVVY Mom likes uses the following sites most often.

Flying to an alternate city or airport in the same region can sometimes save a bundle too. SAVVY Mom and Dad recently flew to Tennessee from Seattle. It turned out they could purchase a first class flight between Seattle and Nashville for the same price as one to Memphis. They flew on the same airline, flight, and day, plus they got the premium seats.

If you decide to try and *Name Your Own Price* be cautious. Priceline, for example, requires you to give them your payment information first. You have to commit sight unseen to the deal if it is accepted. Doing this with rental cars or hotels is not such a bad thing because you can specify the general location of the business or service, and select economy to luxury designations. If however, you want to try and score super cheap airline tickets you may find yourself on the puddle jumping, red-eye flight from Podunk City, Nowhere to Outoftheway Prairie, Nomansland.

www.expedia.com
www.hotels.com
www.mobissimo.com
www.orbitz.com
www.sidestep.com

GIFT GIVING AND REGIFTING THE SAVVY WAY

Holidays, birthdays, weddings, baby showers, graduations, and anniversaries mean lots of potentially expensive gift-giving occasions each year. There is also the potential of those lovely white elephant type goods or gift cards you will never use.

It is ok to re-gift, sell or donate a gift that doesn't suit you, just don't give something back to the original giver. If you can't remember who gave you what make a list or place a note on the item you really don't want or need. This little back-up plan can save you an embarrassing moment at the next gift-giving get-together.

SAVVY Mom once read about a supposed well-meaning boss who gave his employees gift cards instead of a bonus at the holidays. Poor schmuck's wife was a bit unhappy to get a gift card instead of some cash, and when she discovered the gift card was to HOOTERS, she exploded.

If hubby had listened to THE SAVVY CAT he would have sold that unwanted gift card on EBay or traded for something more suitable on one of the many gift card trading websites. Of course he could have done this all before letting the little woman in on the secret.

www.ebay.com
www.giftcardrescue.com

THE SAVVY CAT'S FINAL ADVICE

I dare say this section title seems a bit ominous given my advanced age, but never-the-less I feel the need to sum up the lessons learned as a concluding finale to my savvy monetary advice. Saving money, living within your means, and finding value for your hard-earned cash mean more than ever. Even if the amount of time you have to invest is minimal, adopting a few of these organizational and saving techniques and strategies can help you live smarter, possibly even for less.

Ninety percent of the savings battle is learning to make alternative choices and try new things. You may surprise yourself and find some products you truly love, retailers you never tried, or community services that can help improve your life. Flexibility and consistency are central to my success, and those principles can help you too.

I hope you find some new ideas to try. Pay if forward and share what works for you and yours with others. Purrhaps, we can even start a money-saving crusade. Check out my website at www.thesavvycat.com. You can share your tips and success stories and I can continue to pontificate on matters monetary. I like to think this of a stab at immortality, my visage surfing across the world-wide-web to eternity. That plus a granite statue housing my ashes should keep me in the loop for years to come.

Meows, swats and good luck,

Dr. Cashman, THE SAVVY CAT

ONLINE RESOURCES

The SAVVY Cat utilizes the following websites most frequently when looking for info on the world-wide-web. The list represents a drop in the bucket of potentially helpful sites out there. Inclusion herein does not imply my endorsement of them or their endorsement of me. You will likely find many other sites just as useful. Share what you find with others and we can all benefit. THE SAVVY CAT

AUTOMOTIVE
>aaa.com
>carfax.com
>carinsurance.com
>cars.com
>edmunds.com
>leasetrader.com
>motoralley.com

BUDGETING
>aetv.com/bigspender
>betterbudgeting.com
>clarkhoward.com
>financialplan.about.com
>wesabe.com

EDUCATION/COLLEGE
>upromise.com

EMERGENCY PREPARATION
>fema.gov

FINANCE
>bankrate.com
>bad-credit-advisor.com
>ckfraud.org/chexsystems.html
>fdic.gov

www.thesavvycat.com

ftc.gov
myfico.com

GAS PRICE COMPARISON
gasbuddy.com
mapquest.com

GROCERY SAVINGS/COUPONS
coupons.com
eversave.com
mygrocerydeals.coms
mysavings.com
shortcuts.com/stores
smartsource.com
thecouponclippers.com

HOUSING
apartments.com
craigslist.org
rent.com

INCOME & TAXES
irs.gov

LOCAL/REGIONAL SAVINGS
entertainment.com
restaurant.com
shoplocal.com
valpak.com

LOWERING BILLS
energystar.gov
frugalliving.about.com
savemoney.com
saylowerbills.com

whitefence.com

MEDICAL INSURANCE/PRESCRIPTIONS
commhealth.org
dol.gov
pparx.org

ONLINE SHOPPING
dealhunting.com
fatwallet.com
paypal.com
savings-center.com
slickdeals.net

PHOTOS/PRINTING ONLINE
photoworks.com
vistaprint.com

POSTAL DEALS
usps.com

PRICE COMPARISON
bizrate.com
pricegrabber.com
pricescan.com
shopzilla.com

REBATES/REWARDS
dealhack.com
ebates.com
erewards.com
fatwallet.com
freeafter.com
mypoints.com
refundsweepers.com

SENIOR CONSUMERS
>   aarp.org

TRAVEL
>   aaa.com
>   expedia.com
>   hotels.com
>   mobissimo.com
>   orbitz.com
>   priceline.com
>   sidestep.com

USED/RESALE
>   craigslist.org
>   ebay.com
>   giftcardrescue.com

NOTES:

123 | P a g e

ENDNOTES

[1] http://wuzzle.org/cave/catbits.html 03/09/2009
[2] http:// http://www.irs.gov/pub/irs-pdf/p969.pdf 03/09/2009
[3] http://www.bankrate.com/brm/news/pf/20060215b1.asp 03/09/2009
[4] http://www.irs.gov/retirement/participant/article/0,,id=151786,00.html
[5] www.ckfraud.org 03/09/2009
[6] http://www.bad-credit-advisor.com/what-is-fico-score.html 03/09/2009
[7] http://ficoforums.myfico.com/fico/board/message?board.id=bankruptcy&thread.id=2307 03/09/2009
[8] http://www.ftc.gov/bcp/edu/pubs/consumer/credit/cre18.shtm 03/092009
[9] http://www.ftc.gov/bcp/edu/pubs/consumer/credit/cre18.shtm 03/09/2009
[10] http://www.paws.org/cas/resources/fact_sheets_general/spayneuter.php 03/09/2009

401(k) Resource Guide - Plan Participants - Limitation on Elective Deferrals. (2009, January 1). Retrieved March 11, 2009, from irs.gov: http://www.irs.gov/retirement/participant/article/0,,id=151786,00.html

A.P. Associated Press. (2008, 08 14). *Consumer prices shot up in July.* Retrieved 08 14, 2008, from MSNBC Business: Stocks/Economy: http://www.msnbc.msn.com/id/26195964

Debt Collection FAQs: A Guide for Consumers. (2009, February). Retrieved March 11, 2009, from ftc.gov: http://www.ftc.gov/bcp/edu/pubs/consumer/credit/cre18.shtm

Dept. of Treasury Internal Revenue Service. (2008). *Publication 969 Health Savings Accounts and other Tax-Advantaged Health Plans.* Retrieved March 9, 2009, from irs.gov: http://www.irs.gov/pub/irs-pdf/p969.pdf

How to Select a Legitimate Credit Counseling Agency. (2008, July 11). Retrieved March 11, 2009, from MyFico.com: http://ficoforums.myfico.com/fico/board/message?board.id=bankruptcy&thread.id=2307

Jenny C. McCune. (2006, February 15). *How Long to Keep Financial Records.* Retrieved March 8, 2009, from www.bankrate.com: http://www.bankrate.com/brm/news/pf/20060215b1.asp

National Check Fraud Center. (2006). *National Check Fraud Center ChexSystems Information and Guide.* Retrieved March 09, 2009, from ckfraud.org: http://www.ckfraud.org/chexsystems.html

Progressive Animal Welfare Society. (2009). *Spay and Neuter Resources.* Retrieved March 11, 2009, from Paws.org:
http://www.paws.org/cas/resources/fact_sheets_general/spayneuter.php

REUTERS. (2008, 08 14). *Business/ Mortgage Mess Home foreclosure filings up 55 percent in July.* Retrieved 08 14, 2008, from MSNBC.COM: http://www.msnbc.msn.com/id/26194917

Tidbits of Cat Mythology and Folklore from Various Cultures. (n.d.). Retrieved January 11, 2009, from Cave of the Word Witch: http://wuzzle.org/cave/catbits.html

What is FICO Score? (2003 InfoWeb Inc). Retrieved March 09, 2009, from www.bad-credit-advisor.com: http://www.bad-credit-advisor.com/what-is-fico-score.html

www.ingramcontent.com/pod-product-compliance
Lightning Source LLC
Chambersburg PA
CBHW081133170526
45165CB00008B/2652